TEACH US TO PRAY

Dear Kevin Chang :

Hope you become a prayer!

Ben & Sharon
5 March, 2083

Lord, teach us to pray ...

—Luke 11:1

TEACH US TO PRAY

Stephen Kaung

Christian Fellowship Publishers, Inc.
New York

Paperback ISBN: 978-1-680621-19-8
eBook ISBN: 978-1-68062-120-4

Available from the Publishers at:

11515 Allecingie Parkway
Richmond, Virginia 23235
www.c-f-p.com

Printed in the United States of America

Preface

"... Lord, teach us to pray ..." Luke 11:1

As the Lord's people, the church is called to pray—it is a calling, a right, and a great privilege. There is no calling or power greater than prayer. Prayer links the church to God. "Let thy will be done as in heaven so upon the earth."

When the Lord burdens our heart to pray, we soon realize that we do not know how—it is not in us to pray. It causes us to turn to our Lord and cry out: "Lord, teach us to pray; we need to learn to take up Your burdens; teach us."

In Richmond, Virginia, from February 1981 through October 1982, Stephen Kaung gave a series of messages on corporate prayer. During this period, he shared at the beginning of prayer meetings held every Wednesday evening. These spoken messages have been transcribed into this book. The spoken form has been preserved with only necessary editing for clarity. Some of the matters discussed for prayer are specific to the saints praying in Richmond; however, they are included because they contain principles that could be of help to all God's people.

Contents

1—Teach Us to Pray

Luke 11:1—And it came to pass as he was in a certain place praying, when he ceased, one of his disciples said to him, Lord, teach us to pray, even as John also taught his disciples.

One day the Lord was praying in a certain place, and when He finished, one of the disciples (in a sense, representing all) asked Him: "Lord, teach us to pray." Evidently, when our Lord was praying, His disciples sensed something about His prayer, which was very different from what they had heard or known, or been taught in the past. Otherwise, they would not have asked such a question.

His prayers were so different from those of the scribes and Pharisees and from those of John the Baptist because most of these disciples were previously with John. Apparently, John the Baptist taught them how to pray; but since the Lord's prayer was very, very different, it made a deep impression upon the disciples, causing them to feel they did not know how to pray.

I think the first lesson we must learn in prayer is this: We do not know how to pray. We think we do because we were taught even before we were saved, and since being saved, we have been praying all these years—both privately and together. This develops a kind of confidence in us, causing us to think we know how to pray, but if we were to hear the Lord pray, our first reaction would be that we have never prayed before. We do not know how to pray, and we must ask the Lord to teach us.

Sometimes we believe our problem is that we do not know how to pray; therefore, we dare not pray. Actually, the problem is just the opposite. It is because we know how to pray that our prayer is so ineffective. If we realize we do not know how to pray, then the Lord will teach us, and then our prayers will become real prayers. I think most brothers and sisters do not pray because they feel they do not know how. I feel you should thank the Lord for this because if you know that you do not know how to pray, then there is hope. However, if we think we know how to pray, then we are finished. The Lord will let us pray our prayers because He will not be able to teach us.

We probably do not realize how insufficient and weak we are in this matter of prayer because we have not heard the Lord pray. It is not only the content of His prayer that is different but also its very spirit. We have to come to Him and say, "Lord, teach us to pray."

We must learn the following things: (1) We must confess that we do not know how to pray, and it must be a deep confession. (2) We must *want* to pray. If we have this desire, then we are teachable. When we come together for prayer, many have already decided they will not pray. (3) We must ask the Lord to teach us to pray. We must look away from ourselves unto Him, that He may open our hearts and spirits, and say: "Lord, we are willing; we want to pray, but we do not know how. Please teach us." As we begin to come into the good of these three things, we will hear the Lord say, "When you pray ..." In other words, the Lord will teach you.

Remember the story about the Pharisee and the publican. When the Pharisee came to the temple, he surely knew how to pray a very long and complete prayer. The publican did not know how to pray or even where to begin, so he just cried out from his heart, "O God, have compassion on me, the sinner." The Lord's reply was, "This man went down to his house justified rather than the other" (Luke 18:13-14).

I do hope that we do not come together with a sense of confidence in ourselves; but rather, we come knowing our weakness. In Romans 8, we are told that the Holy Spirit will come to our aid, helping us in our weakness, making intercession in us and for us according to God's will. The Holy Spirit knows the mind of God. In consideration of these things, I do encourage you that your not knowing does not inhibit your praying. It should rather encourage you to pray. When we come together for prayer, we need to keep our hearts and spirits open to Him. When a subject for prayer is mentioned, just ask the Lord whether He wants you to pray and if you feel He does, then trust the Holy Spirit to give you the right words. As you do this, it becomes very easy and very natural. This is the first lesson, and I hope we all learn it.

2—Prayer and Burden

Matthew 9:35-38—And Jesus went round all the cities and the villages, teaching in their synagogues, and preaching the glad tidings of the kingdom, and healing every disease and every bodily weakness. But when he saw the crowds he was moved with compassion for them, because they were harassed, and cast away as sheep not having a shepherd. Then saith he to his disciples, The harvest is great and the workmen are few, supplicate therefore the Lord of the harvest, that he send forth workmen unto his harvest.

Our Lord went around the cities and villages teaching, preaching, and healing. As He was doing that, He saw the crowds and was moved with compassion. In His vision, He saw them as sheep without a shepherd, and because of this, He was deeply burdened and moved with compassion. He shared His vision with His disciples, and He said, "The harvest is great and the workmen are few; supplicate therefore the Lord of the harvest, that he send forth workmen unto his harvest." If we see as the Lord sees and have a vision that He reveals to us, it will constitute a burden in us. When there is this burden, the only way to discharge it is through prayer. Oftentimes, when we pray either individually or together, we think we cannot pray because we have no burden. Now it is true that prayer without a burden is not a real prayer. We must pray with burden, but if we say because we have no burden, therefore, we cannot pray, then something is wrong.

Why do we not have burden? I think there are several reasons:

(1) We do not see. The disciples were with the Lord and saw the crowds, but they had no vision. In their seeing the crowds, they did not see them as sheep without a shepherd. They only saw the crowds outwardly. Inwardly, they could not see the need, and lacking this vision, they were not burdened. Since the disciples were not burdened and moved with compassion, the Lord had to share with them in order to get them to pray. Today, we are not alert and spiritually sensitive. We are dull. If our spirit is really open to the Lord, then we will find it is very easy to see what the Lord sees and be burdened with His burden.

(2) We are overburdened with our own problems and needs. When we are fully occupied with the problems of our immediate family, we have no strength to take up more burden. Therefore, if we want to really enter into this matter of intercession, we must first have our spirits open, being alert and sensitive so the Lord may be able to share His burden with us and impress upon us the need that He sees.

(3) As we come to pray, we need to set aside our own burdens, at least temporarily. We should not come over-burdened or with heavy loads upon our spirits. Yes, we do have our problems, but because we want to enter into this matter of intercession, we have to forget and lay aside our personal needs temporarily. Then we can come with openness and emptiness that we might be able to take on burdens from the Lord.

We need to have a burden in prayer, but it is not something for which we wait until it comes upon us. Probably, that is a problem among God's people. When we come together, we just wait because we feel we have no burden. We wait until the burden comes, and then we pray. In one sense, we cannot pray without burden, but it is not something for which we wait passively until it falls upon us. It is something which we have to take up actively. I think the secret of prayer is that we know how to take up a burden voluntarily and actively, not waiting for it to come upon us passively and involuntarily.

In this passage, when the Lord shared His vision and burden with His disciples, He commanded them to pray. In other words, the Lord expected them to take up His vision and burden and turn them into prayer. Evidently, they prayed, and the more they prayed, the more they were burdened. Perhaps, in the beginning, they were just taking up the Lord's burden; but the burden increased within them as they continued to pray. They really prayed with burden. How do we know this? In Matthew 10, we find this word: "And having called to him his twelve disciples, he gave them power over unclean spirits, so that they should cast them out, and heal every disease and every bodily weakness" (v. 1). The Lord sent them out, and their prayers were answered. They had prayed that the Lord of the harvest would send forth workmen, and the Lord sent them forth. Prayer was answered!

Sometimes, when we come together, and there are matters being mentioned for prayer, probably, some of us will say: "I do not feel burdened about these matters. I am burdened about others. If they are mentioned, I will pray." In your personal prayer, this may be true; but in corporate prayer, you cannot go on this rule. In corporate prayer, we are to lay aside all other burdens because we are not coming to pray our own burden. No! We should lay that aside. We come here with openness and emptiness, ready to take up burdens, and only then can we pray corporately. Therefore, when the subjects are mentioned, be open and learn to take them up actively. I believe if we start to take them up, we will be burdened.

There is another problem. I wonder if you notice when we come to pray for a certain one who is sick or who has some difficulties and we know them very well, it seems as if many of brothers and sisters will pray. But when we mention something about the Lord's work or interest, somehow, we shut up because we feel we are not burdened. Is it because we are limited by our emotions? Must we be emotionally involved to receive a burden? Or can we pray above our emotions and learn to take up the Lord's burden until we find ourselves really burdened?

In learning to take up these burdens, it cannot be done instantaneously. It is something to be learned in our daily lives. When we see, hear or read about something, try to take it up as a burden and turn it into prayer. Suppose we meet someone who shares something with us. After they leave, we can learn to turn that encounter into prayer. Perhaps we are reading the newspaper, and we find something there—we can take it up and turn it into prayer. If we are watchful and alert in our daily life, learning to take up burdens and converting them into prayers, I believe we will learn the secret of taking up burdens. Then when we come together and certain things are mentioned, it will not be hard for us to enter into prayer for these things.

Of course, we need a certain amount of knowledge in order to pray intelligently. Therefore, it is always good when a certain thing is mentioned in the church to have it explained very briefly. In other words, give enough information so that all the brothers and sisters can really enter in. For instance, when a person's name or a certain thing is mentioned, some may be familiar with it, but the rest are not. So it would be good to have a little information that others might understand and learn to take up that burden.

We want all the brothers and sisters to learn to pray, and, as we mentioned last time, if you do not know how to pray, then you should pray. If you know how to pray, then probably, you should not. Let's come with openness, and when things are mentioned for prayer, look to the Lord and take up whatever burden He has for you. Pray a sentence or two, or if you feel you want to pray more, it is all right. It is not in the words, whether they are many or few. You know that the Lord knows, so just pray as He enables you.

3—If Two Shall Agree

Matthew 18:19—Again I say to you, that if two of you shall agree on the earth concerning any matter, whatsoever it may be that they shall ask, it shall come to them from my Father who is in the heavens.

Our Lord Jesus is speaking these words to us, and no doubt, this verse applies to corporate prayer because it says, "if two of you," and we know two is the smallest of plurality. It may be two, it may be twenty, it may be two hundred, it may be two thousand or more. In other words, it is not just one person praying; it is two or more praying together.

For corporate prayer to be effective, there is a basic requirement. What the Lord mentioned in this verse is of unlimited scope because He said, "concerning any matter, whatsoever it may be that they shall ask." We can pray for any and everything, and the promise is very inclusive—His Father will answer us. However, there is one condition, and that is, "agree." When we come together to pray, it is different from private or personal prayer. There is an added dimension to it because not only must there be agreement between you and the Lord but also between you and your brothers and sisters.

"If two of you shall agree ..." How can we agree? As a matter of fact, no two persons can agree on anything. In the final analysis, I think you will find it is true that no person can really agree because everyone has their own self; and as long as that self is there, you want people to agree with you. We may come to an agreement by negotiation or compromise, but this is not what the Lord is talking about. The word agree in the original means "symphonize," such as in an orchestra where there are many and various instruments. It is not uniformity because there are all kinds of instruments, and each has its specific tone. As these different instruments are played, there are no jarring or discordant sounds. On the contrary, the sounds all blend together into one. This is the meaning of the word agree, as it is used here. It is not in the sense that everyone is repeating the same thing—that would be vain repetition.

When we are praying together, some will have one approach or emphasis, and others will have another. Everyone can pray as the Lord leads, and the prayers will merge together into one. Now how can it be possible? In an orchestra, it is possible because there is a conductor and everyone has to lay down himself and follow the conductor. To put it another way, everyone must agree with the conductor and not just with the person next to him. All eyes are upon the conductor, and it is through him that the musical instruments can play together in perfect harmony. This is a secret of corporate prayer. Our conductor is our Lord Jesus through His Holy Spirit. We do believe that when we come together to pray, He is here because, in the next verse, it says: "For where two or three are gathered together unto my name, there am I in the midst of them" (v.20).

We are just like those in an orchestra, each waiting upon the Lord with a different instrument, playing according to what the Lord has enabled us. Everyone must lay himself down—his opinion, his prejudice, his inclination, his choice—and as we do, we will agree with the Lord. The Lord does not require that you agree with me or vice versa because even if we try, it will not be real. All He requires is that everyone agree with Him, looking to Him to direct them; then we shall play our instruments in harmony. Sometimes, all the musical instruments are played; at other times, some are waiting. Nevertheless, it is all under the direction of the conductor, and it will come forth as beautiful music.

Corporate prayer is not cheap at all. It is costly! In corporate prayer, we just cannot pray as we want or do not want. Everybody must be ready and open, waiting for the conductor to direct us, and then we will pray according to the Spirit of God that is within us. As we lay ourselves down and are open to the Holy Spirit, we will find our prayers blending together in agreement; and there is power there.

You remember in the book of Acts how the 120 people waited upon the Lord, praying with one accord. There were 120 opinions and ideas, but they were able to pray with one accord because everyone was tuned to the Lord.

Later on, we see the church prayed with one voice, the place shook, and the Lord gave them boldness to witness for Him. There is tremendous power in corporate prayer.

As we pray together, first of all, let us lay down ourselves. Do not decide whether you will pray or not, but be ready and open. After a matter is mentioned, do not immediately draw a conclusion as to how it should be prayed. Wait upon the Lord and, as He moves upon your spirit, then pray accordingly. If we are open to the Lord in this way, our prayers will be *symphonized* together with one accord, and this is the way the Lord will answer our prayers. May we remember this.

4—Prayer and Faith

James 1:5-8—But if any one of you lack wisdom, let him ask of God, who gives to all freely and reproaches not, and it shall be given to him: but let him ask in faith, nothing doubting. For he that doubts is like a wave of the sea driven by the wind and tossed about; for let not that man think that he shall receive anything from the Lord; he is a double-minded man, unstable in all his ways.

"Ask in faith, nothing doubting." I hope we all know that one of the most basic rules in prayer is faith, whether it is our private, personal prayer, or corporate prayer. Without faith, we cannot please God. In Hebrews, we read: "For he that draws near to God must believe that he is, and that he is a rewarder of them who seek him out" (Hebrews 11:6). When we come to prayer, we must come to God, believing that He is the great I AM, and He is One who rewards those who seek Him.

Oftentimes, we come to pray, but somehow we do not ask in faith; rather, we doubt in our heart. Probably, it is because we try to bring God into our limitations. In other words, when we ask Him for something which we can do, we believe He can do it; but when we ask something that is beyond our ability, then we begin to doubt whether He is able to hear us. We seem to be the scope or limitation of our prayers. As we come to pray, we have to get out of ourselves and our limitations and set our eyes upon the Lord.

Notice what is said here: "Let him ask of God, who gives to all freely and reproaches not." Sometimes, we dare not ask because we do not believe that He gives freely to all. We think we do not deserve it, we have not earned it, or our work is not done sufficiently. Therefore, we do not come to Him and ask. We need to see that our God is One who loves to give, and He gives to all freely. This is the God to whom we come! We do not come to a God who requires from us certain conditions, works, or merits before He will hear us. We come to a God who reproaches not. Sometimes, we dare not pray because we think if we pray wrongly, He may reproach us. But it says "reproaches not." *We may pray wrongly, but He will answer rightly.* He will not reproach us because we pray wrongly. So dear brothers and sisters, as we come to pray, if we set our eyes upon Him and not ourselves, that will give us liberty and courage to pray. Just remember that we ask of God who gives to all freely and reproaches not. This is the God to whom we come. Now, ask in faith.

Of course, if we know what His will is and pray according to that will, then we have the confidence that He hears us. But sometimes, we do not know what His will is. Is it because of our not knowing that we cannot ask in faith? Probably, we think that asking in faith means believing in the thing for which we ask, but that is not so. Asking in faith is believing that He hears us. Our faith is not in the thing for which we pray. Our faith is in the God of whom we ask.

Now, what is faith? Sometimes, we think it is our believing the thing is of God, or that we already have it, and then it will be ours; but that is putting our faith in the thing instead of in God. That is not where our faith anchors. It anchors in God. We believe that He gives to all freely and reproaches not. We believe He loves to hear our prayers and knows how to answer rightly, even if we pray wrongly. Now that is where our faith is, and because we believe in Him, we ask in faith, nothing doubting. We do not doubt that God will hear us. We do not doubt that He knows just what is best for us. He knows what answer to give, whether it is yes or no. Therefore, if we set our face towards the Lord, remembering who He is and what a God He is to us, then we can ask in faith. We believe Him and do not doubt that He hears us.

"For he that doubts is like a wave of the sea driven by the wind and tossed about; for let not that man think that he shall receive anything from the Lord; he is a double-minded man, unstable in all his ways" (James 1:6b,7-8).

This means that if we doubt Him, then we will get nothing because we are a double-minded person. In the original, it says a double-soul man. In other words, we set our heart on the Lord and also on something else, with wicked eyes—double eyes. And a double-minded man will not be able to get anything from God.

I think there is a good illustration of this in the Bible. Do you remember when our Lord came down from the Mount of Transfiguration and was met by a father who had a son troubled by a dumb spirit? The disciples were not able to cast out the demon, and the father came to the Lord, saying, "But if thou couldst do anything, be moved with pity on us, and help us." The Lord replied, "The `if thou couldst' is [if thou couldst] believe: all things are possible to him that believes. And immediately the father of the young child crying out said with tears, I believe, help mine unbelief" (Mark 9:22b, 23-24). He did not have that faith in the Lord. He was wondering if the Lord could do anything. He was limiting the

27

Lord by himself and by the disciples. So the Lord put it back to him in the form of a question, saying: "Do not ask if I can. Ask yourself the question 'if you could believe;' because all things are possible to him who believes." When the father cried out for help, he was saying there must be some kind of unbelief in him because he was trying to limit the Lord, to circumscribe Him and bring Him down to his level. "Help my unbelief. Take it away that I might believe You are able to do anything." Because the father believed, the Lord cast the demon out.

As we come together to pray, let us ask in faith, nothing doubting. It does not mean we put our faith in the thing for which we ask. Oftentimes, people will say, "You must believe." Now, what should we believe? We believe in God; we do not believe in the thing. That is where our faith is, and if we believe in God, it is easy. If we try to believe in the thing, it is very difficult. If we believe in God and ask in faith, nothing doubting, then the Lord will reveal His mind to us, and He will answer our prayer. This must be true whether we are praying alone or together. It is a basic rule for prayer.

May the Lord help us and give us that confidence in Him. How can we doubt Him? How can we be afraid of asking Him? He is just waiting to give freely, and He will never reproach us. Don't be afraid; just open your mouth, and let's pray together.

5—Authoritative Prayer

Isaiah 45:11—Thus saith Jehovah, the Holy One of Israel, and his Maker: Ask me of the things to come; concerning my sons, and concerning the work of my hands, command ye me.

Here our God is calling us to ask of Him. Sometimes we wonder why it is that God should ever call us to ask of Him. Certainly, we will ask Him. We do not need to be asked to ask Him. But here, it is said to "ask of Me" as if we are not asking.

Now the Bible says you have not because you ask not. Why do we not ask? Probably, we do not trust Him, or sometimes, we are just indifferent; we do not feel there is anything to ask. So the Lord calls us to ask Him.

Prayer is a calling. We are called to pray, and not to pray is a sin. I believe we all have to acknowledge that we have committed this sin very frequently. We ought to ask—ask of Him—but we do not. We either try ourselves, or we are just not concerned. The sin of prayerlessness is a very real sin, and we should remember that we are called by God to pray. He calls us to ask of Him. Therefore, He is waiting to hear us.

Notice it says, "Ask me of the things to come." Now, what are the things to come? It is qualified by: "Concerning my sons, and concerning the work of my hands." We are to ask Him of the things that concern God's children or things that concern the work of His hands. God is very interested in His people. His desire is to have His Son formed in us that He may lead many sons into glory. This is God's will and eternal purpose. But what do we see today? What are the actual conditions of God's people? We see many babies. We are not growing up as we should. There is very little sonship manifested in our lives. How anxious and concerned our heavenly Father must be. He wants us to be sons so that His only begotten Son may be the firstborn among His many brethren. That is God's supreme desire, His concern, and He calls us to ask Him about this. This is "the things to come."

We know that one day when the sons of God shall be manifested, even this universe will be delivered from bondage and corruption and will enter into the liberty of the sons of God. How can these things be? It is because of the work of His hands. In the original, the word work is "the finished work." He said, "Concerning my sons and concerning the finished work of my hands." If the work is already finished, why should we ask? But because it is finished, we have to ask. When our Lord Jesus was on the cross, He said, "It is finished." The work of redemption is finished, so far as God is concerned, and on the basis of the finished work, the Holy Spirit is able to work it in us to make us sons of God. God calls us to ask concerning the finished work of His hands. Two thousand years ago, He finished something. But two thousand years later, it is still unfinished in us, and certainly, this is something that we should ask for Him to complete. He has already begun the good work in us. Shall He not complete it? He is waiting for us to ask Him about these things.

Oftentimes, we ask about the things which interest us and do not ask of the things which interest Him. Are we concerned with His concern? Are we burdened with His burden that all His people may reach maturity? He has already begun a good work in all of us because whom He has foreknown, He has called. He has already called us. Whom He has called, He has justified. He has already justified us. Whom He has justified, He has glorified. Has He glorified us? He has predestinated us to be conformed to the image of His Son. It can be done because the work is finished, and this ought to occupy our mind and our thinking and be our prayer.

When we come together, we are not just coming to pray in a very vague, abstract, general way. We have a work to do—to pray that the finished work of Christ may be fully realized among His people. The scope of our prayer is almost unlimited. We are not limited to praying for ourselves and our families. Actually, the scope of our prayer includes all of God's people, His eternal purpose, and His finished work. Whether we are praying for things, individuals, or companies of believers, remember that the basis of all our prayers is "concerning my sons and concerning the work of my hands."

God is anxious about this (not in the sense of being worried such as we do) and wants it very much. Therefore, He calls us to ask Him about it. If we do not ask, it is as if God's hands are tied. In this work, He needs our cooperation, which is primarily to pray. He gets so anxious that you find He not only calls us to ask Him but concludes with, "Command ye me." Now isn't that irreverent? How can we command God? He commands us, and when He does, we must obey and follow. But here, He gives us permission to command Him. Of course, we must be careful and let no flesh come in, thinking we are greater than God. We must remember it is the Greater who commands. This permission that He gives us is called authoritative prayer. It is the prayer of command. When you think of asking, you are praying upward. When you think of commanding, you are praying downward. In other words, you take up a heavenly position (which God has given to you in Christ, you are seated with Him who is above), praying from heaven to earth.

"Whatsoever ye shall bind on the earth shall be bound in heaven, and whatsoever ye shall loose on the earth shall be loosed in heaven" (Matthew 18:18).

God has given us the privilege and right of asking Him because we are His children. If we are strangers, we cannot ask of Him since we do not have the right; He will not hear us. We must remember we are God's children and have this right and privilege and come to our heavenly Father and ask of Him. Do not be afraid. But even better than asking as children, we, as His servants, can command Him. Usually, a servant is given a command to follow, but we, as servants, have been given the authority to command Him because He has already revealed His mind to us; and when we command Him, we only command Him to do what He wants. He wants it so much that He asks us to command it and not just say, "Lord, please do," but, "Lord, You must do it because this is Your will; this is Your purpose; this is Your desire; this is what Christ has already done on the cross." Now that is the prayer of command.

Of course, if you do not know the will of God, you cannot pray the prayer of command. That would be presumption. We only have the authority to command Him as He reveals His mind to us. After He has revealed His mind to us, our prayer is no longer one of pleading but one of command. So we can see how anxious God is that we pray this kind of prayer because this is something which is very, very dear to His heart. He wants to see His children fully matured, conformed to the image of His Son. He wants to see the finished work of Christ fully realized in the lives of those whom He has called.

We see from all of this that prayer is more than just prayer. It is really working together with God for His purpose to be soon realized. Let us come with humility and yet with boldness.

6 – Prayer for Those in Authority

I Timothy 2:1-4 — I exhort therefore, first of all, that
supplications, prayers, intercessions, thanksgivings be
made for all men; for kings and all that are in dignity,
that we may lead a quiet and tranquil life in all piety
and gravity; for this is good and acceptable before our
Saviour God, who desires that all men should be saved
and come to the knowledge of the truth.

When Paul exhorted Timothy, actually, he exhorted the
whole church. In other words, the Spirit of God through Paul
exhorts us that we supplicate, pray, and intercede for all men.
The ministry of the church is prayer. There is no greater
ministry than this calling of the church to pray for all men.

Sometimes we find it difficult to pray because we are not
of this world, yet we are in it. The Lord has called us out of
the world and delivered us from it. We do not belong to the
world anymore. We have been set apart as a people by God,
and we should not identify ourselves with the world or be
entangled by its affairs. Because we do not belong to this
world as a system, we are not called by God to reform it or to
make it a better place. While on earth, our Lord Jesus did not
reform or change the world in the physical or material sense.

We are not of this world, and yet we are in it since the
Lord has not yet taken us to himself. Thank God, He is going
to take us to himself. But at present, we are still here, and as
strangers and sojourners, we are to be the salt of the earth and
the light of the world. Our very presence in this world is to

serve as a restraining power against corruption and evil. There is a phrase in II Thessalonians 2:7 which says "he who restrains." (I am not interpreting it; I am just using it.) That is the church as the salt of the earth. We are to serve as a kind of preservative to keep it from further corruption. We are to offer to this world the standard of right and wrong. The world is in total darkness and cannot see the difference between right and wrong. The church is the light that should shine.

Now how do we reconcile these two almost opposite positions—our not being of the world and yet we are in the world to serve as salt and light? To complicate the situation, there is the problem that whatever happens in the world affects us. Suppose there is a war and we are in the war zone, or we are living under a government that is anti-God. Is there a way to live as not of the world yet in the world serving as salt and light? I think the way is here. We are called to pray, supplicate and intercede. Now, these words—prayers, supplications, and intercessions—cannot be completely isolated from each other, but they do give the full meaning of prayers. When there is supplication, the emphasis is on our personal needs. Prayer is of a more general term, more inclusive. In intercession, the emphasis is on taking up the needs of others and bringing them to God because we have access to Him.

We are exhorted to pray in different ways to bring all of these matters to God. The scope is so broad that He says to pray for all men and not just our immediate circle because God is interested in all men. We are exhorted to pray for kings and those in dignity. In other words, we are to pray for those in authority. Let's look at the two reasons given:

(1) "That we may lead a quiet and tranquil life in all piety and gravity." Through prayer, we will be granted such an environment that we might lead a quiet life. This world is not friendly to us because we do not belong. It is even hostile to our spiritual life. Everything in this world is against our spiritual growth. It is not conducive to us. We are living in such a difficult environment; therefore, we need to pray for all men, and especially those in authority, because they can affect our lives to a very large degree. In a sense, they can provide us with the right or wrong environment. We must pray that the Lord will rule over their lives, overruling them, so they will not make our environment worse. This is a very humble prayer. We are not super in any way, but we cry to the Lord, "Lead us not into temptation but deliver us from the evil one." When we pray for all men and those in authority, it is actually asking God not to lead us into temptation and to deliver us from the evil one, that He might provide us with an environment in which we can live godly before Him.

(2) "For this is good and acceptable before our Saviour God, who desires that all men should be saved and come to the knowledge of the truth." In the first instance where we are praying for all men, we are praying for ourselves, which might seem selfish, but it is really that we may live a life that is pleasing to God and for His glory. As we pray for all men and those in authority, we are praying according to the will of God, who would have all men be saved and come to the knowledge of Him. Unless the church prays, they will not be given the opportunity to be saved. So that is the second reason we should pray for all men and those in authority.

Let's look at these words in Romans 13: "For there is no authority except from God; and those that exist are set up by

God. For rulers are not a terror to a good work, but to an evil one. For it is God's minister to thee for good" (vv.1b, 3a, 4a).

It is God who sets up all authority upon this earth. We have government and also those who rule over us. Authorities are appointed by God for one purpose: to punish evil and protect the good. Although today we find authorities are doing just the opposite, this is still the basic meaning of God's setting up authorities on this earth. They have the power to do the will of God. Therefore, it behooves us to pray for them. God has allowed them to be there, and we must pray that they truly be His ministers and not the ministers of the enemy. We must ask God to touch their hearts and move them to do the right thing, that they would be exercising justice to see that the evil is punished and the good is protected. We need to pray for them that they may serve God and His purpose.

To put it in another way: God has not called us to reform the world. (Now, one day our Lord Jesus will come, and when He does, He will not reform it, He will change it, bringing His own kingdom upon this earth.) I believe He wants us to touch the world, not directly but indirectly, through prayer. There is no power greater than prayer! Sometimes, we think that if we don't plunge into the world system and try to change things, then we won't be able to live here. But we forget there is a power that is greater than our direct intervention; it is the power of prayer. Why is this so? Because when we pray, it is God who touches the situation instead of ourselves. Sometimes, we forget and think prayer is of no use and we must do something directly. But prayer is more powerful than any activity we can be engaged in. It is the greatest power the church has.

Queen Mary of Scotland once said she was not afraid of the armies of Scotland, but she was afraid of the prayers of John Knox. When John Knox was on his knees, Queen Mary trembled.

How powerful is prayer, and this is a power that we fail to exercise. We forget to exercise it, but we are exhorted to use that power. Only in this manner will we be able to maintain the balance—being in the world, yet not of it. By prayer alone, we are able to control situations and the environment around us. We do not touch them directly. We go through the throne and let the throne touch it. I believe this is far better.

In summary, I believe this is the way that we should pray: Pray for all men, especially those in authority. In that way, we are able to restrain the evil before its time, and we are enabled to stand for the will of God to be accomplished in this world—whether national, international, or local. I feel the Lord wants us to use this power in the right way. We are not directly involved with the world system because we are not of the world. Yet God has put us here with a purpose, and the way to fulfill it is through the ministry of prayer.

In view of what has just recently happened (referring to the attempted assassination of President Reagan), probably, the Lord is reminding us that we really need to pray for those in authority. We really need to pray that God will use them to do His will and provide us with the right environment so we may continue to live a tranquil life in all godliness.

It is true, and we are very thankful to the Lord that we are still free to worship and meet together. However, in this country, as far as the environment is concerned, it is not good. It is very difficult to live a godly life. We must pray that the

Lord will control all the decisions of the government in order that evil will be restrained, that there will be the opportunity to bring the gospel to all men, and that God will still give us an opportunity to live in a way that will be pleasing to Him.

7—Persistent Prayer

Luke 18:1-8—And he spoke also a parable to them to the purport that they should always pray and not faint, saying, There was a judge in a city, not fearing God and not respecting man: and there was a widow in that city, and she came to him, saying, Avenge me of mine adverse party. And he would not for a time; but afterwards he said within himself, If even I fear not God and respect not man, at any rate because this widow annoys me I will avenge her, that she may not by perpetually coming completely harass me. And the Lord said, Hear what the unjust judge says. And shall not God at all avenge his elect, who cry to him day and night, and he bears long as to them? I say unto you that he will avenge them speedily. But when the Son of man comes, shall he indeed find faith on the earth?

Here we find our Lord teaching His disciples a lesson: They should always pray and not faint. To put it in another way: We should always pray and not give up. Oftentimes, we pray, but we do not continue praying; we give up very quickly. I think there are several reasons: (1) We pray without burden. If we do that, we pray casually and forget quickly. (2) We may have a misconception, thinking that if we pray more than once, it shows a lack of faith. In this passage, probably, the contrary is true. The Lord said, "But when the Son of man comes, shall he indeed find faith on the earth?" That faith is:

This widow prays continuously, persistently, and will not give up until she gets the answer.

It is true, if you pray once and you get the answer, you do not need to pray the second time, and if you pray more, you may lose your faith. On the other hand, if you pray and you do not have the answer, then you should continue on praying, and that is a sign of faith. In other words, you believe the Lord will eventually answer you. I think this is an important principle both in private and corporate prayer. When the church gathers to pray, she takes up burdens from the Lord. Some burdens may be discharged in one session, but others continue on for years; and for this reason, we have to continue to pray.

We cannot pray more than once for anything for which we are not burdened. If we have no burden, the most we can do is to pray just once. If we are really burdened, praying more than once is not a repetition or a monotonous routine; it is real each time. I believe we sometimes find a lack of result in prayer because we give up too quickly.

Notice the instance concerning Abraham when he prayed for the city of Sodom. He did not pray once; he prayed six times. He prayed and prayed and prayed and prayed and prayed and prayed! Remember, our Lord in the garden of Gethsemane prayed three times until He got the answer. You will find the same thing true with Paul. He prayed for the thorn in his flesh three times until he got the answer.

Therefore, it is important for us to know that when we gather together for prayer, there are things for which we must always pray and not give up. We have to continue on until we get the answer.

I like the words in Isaiah 62:6-7: "I have set watchmen upon thy walls, Jerusalem; all the day and all the night they shall never hold their peace: ye that put Jehovah in remembrance, keep not silence, and give him no rest, till he establish, and till he make Jerusalem a praise in the earth."

"For Zion's sake will I not hold my peace, and for Jerusalem's sake I will not be still, until her righteousness go forth as brightness, and her salvation as a torch that burneth" (Isaiah 62:1). God reveals His mind, showing us what He wants, and then in verse 6, He says that for this reason He has set watchmen upon the walls.

When we come together to pray, we are as watchmen being set upon the walls of Jerusalem. He expects us as watchmen not to hold our peace day and night, not to be silent, and to give Him no rest till He makes Jerusalem a city of praise. This is what He wants, and this is what the church should do. The Lord has a mind, a will, a purpose, and a work which He wants to be done, and He sets us as watchmen upon the walls.

In Luke 18, we find a widow who is a type of the church. As far as the church in the world is concerned, she is like a widow because our Lord is absent today, and we are left here helpless and oppressed by our enemy. Satan is the enemy, the adversary of God and man. In this world, we are harassed, oppressed, attacked, assaulted, and tempted by the enemy who is forever trying to frustrate us to prevent our fulfilling God's purpose. We have only one recourse, which is to go to our Judge, and here the Lord used this unjust judge to reveal the righteous Judge, our Lord. This contrast is used to bring out how much more our God and Father will do for us.

This unjust judge had no respect for man and did not fear God. He refused to avenge the widow, but she would not give up. She came and came and came, annoying him until he was so harassed that he said he would do it to keep her from bothering him. Now the Lord said, "And shall not God at all avenge his elect?" It is a contrast to bring out the impact of it, but the lesson is that we are to keep on praying and not give up. That is faith, and with this kind of faith, we will get the answer.

When the same things are mentioned for prayer, I hope we will not feel we are getting rusty. Some things for which we pray, we find that the burden will be gone, and we do not need to go back again. However, there are other things for which the church has to keep on praying and not give up until the Lord does something. May the Lord help us!

8—Intercession

Isaiah 59:16—And he saw that there was no man, and he wondered that there was no intercessor; and his arm brought him salvation, and his righteousness, it sustained him.

Ezekiel 22:30—And I sought for a man among them, that should make up the fence, and stand in the breach before me for the land, that I should not destroy it; but I found none.

In Isaiah 59:16, we see that the Lord is going to do something for His people. He is going to save, deliver and bless them, but before He does it, He looks for a man, an intercessor. His arm is not short that He cannot save, but He is waiting for someone with intercessory prayer to release His arm.

In the passage in Ezekiel, the Lord is going to destroy the land, but this is not His heart's desire. He has to do it because there are certain conditions that require His judgment, but He is very reluctant to do it. He is still looking for someone who will make up the fence and stand in the breach. If He can find someone, He will spare the land. Unfortunately, there is no one.

In these two cases, you can see that whether the Lord is to save or destroy, He is looking for intercessors. An intercessor does not twist God's arm to make Him do what He does not want to do; he is to release the arm of God. He does not pray against God's heart, but he is to open God's heart to His people. An intercessor identifies himself with God and, at the same time, identifies himself with God's people. Identification is the first qualification of an intercessor. If we cannot identify ourselves with God, we cannot intercede; and if we cannot identify ourselves with God's people, again, we cannot be an intercessor. Therefore, in the Scripture, we find that all those who are intercessors identify both with God and man. On the one hand, you stand with God, and on the other with man. An intercessor is not a mediator, but he does identify with both sides. Intercessory prayer is making up the fence and also standing in the breach. In intercessory prayer, repentance is brought in. A broken and contrite spirit is produced, and this is making up the fence and standing in the breach.

A typical case of this is found in the book of Nehemiah. The walls of Jerusalem were broken down, full of breaches and gaps—no separation and no protection—and the people of God suffered affliction. The task of Nehemiah was to rebuild these walls, and in chapter 3, we find it was not a job for one person. God used Nehemiah, but He had to arouse the remnant that was in the Promised Land to work together, each building a section of the wall. As each stood in the gap and worked together, the walls were joined, separation from the world was completed, and the protection was established.

As we gather to pray, brothers and sisters, I feel that we do not just come to attend a prayer meeting. *We come to work!* It is the hardest of all kinds of work. It is the time that we come together as one—not just one person but the many as one. And we try to stand in whatever breach we find and make up the fence. We sympathize with God with whatever His will may be and wherever His heart may lie. Sometimes, God has to do something which is not what He wants, and we have, in a sense, to stand with His heart instead of with His judgment. At other times, God wants to do something, but He is bound; and we need to stand with Him to release His arm.

Thus when we come together, that is what we intend to do as intercessors. We want to identify ourselves with God, with His heart, with His arm, and, of course, we know that His heart and arm are primarily related to His people. The intercessors do touch upon the whole world, but it is basically about His people. Because God's heart is with His people, He wants to bless; He does not want to judge. This is where we must stand. But at the same time, we are His people, so we identify ourselves with them, confessing whatever sins there are and acknowledging there are lots of breaches and gaps. We must not point the finger at others but be identified with God's people.

We see this in Daniel. When he was praying, he identified himself with the children of Israel. He was not involved personally, but in the spirit, he identified himself with them. That is intercessory prayer.

The second qualification of intercessory prayer is agony. Intercessory prayer is very costly. It is not simply that we touch upon something, and whether God hears or not really does not matter. It is real agonizing. It is not something that you try to work up. Some people may feel that we need to agonize and groan, which may become like a habit. That is not the point. It is agony of the heart. We identify ourselves with God and His people to such an extent that we cannot help but feel deeply touched and burdened. That is agony.

In Colossians, we see how Paul strove in prayer even for those whom he had never seen. He identified himself with God in his concern for these Colossian believers. He agonized in prayer for them that God might deliver them from all the distractions and deceptions they were in and bring them back to God's purpose. If we do not know how to bear a burden to the extent of agonizing before God, then we are short of intercessory prayer.

The third thing concerning intercessory prayer is authority. It is different from ordinary prayer because it is authoritative. After we have entered into the burden of the Lord concerning His people and have come to know His mind and will, then it is time to exercise authority before God over whatever condition or situation there may be.

These are the three primary qualifications of intercessory prayer. Therefore, our corporate prayer time is a very serious one. We cannot just come and play, but we need to really give ourselves to the Lord and His people for intercession according to His will. It is a tremendous thing!

The scope of intercession is universal and not limited just to ourselves. Of course, God has put us here, and that should be our burden because the principle is always from "Jerusalem, and in all Judea and Samaria, and to the end of the earth" (Acts 1:8b). No doubt we are to take up the burden for local issues, but we need to go beyond them because God's interest is universal. Therefore, the Lord is looking for a people who will stand in the gap, make up the fence and intercede according to Him.

When I was in grade school, I remember reading a story about a little boy who lived in Holland. The land of Holland is below sea level, so they had to build dikes to hold back the water. If you have ever been there, you know this is true. This little boy was returning home from school, and he noticed on one of the dikes there was a small hole, and the water was seeping through. He realized the consequence would be a flood of the whole country if this small hole was not stopped because it would finally break the dike. He did the only thing he knew to do, which was to put his finger in the hole to stop the leak. I do not remember the entire story, but for us, it points out very vividly the need to stand in the gap. This is what God expects of us. He wants us to stand in the gap so that the enemy will not be able to come in like a flood. Prayer is doing this kind of work, and God is looking for people who will work with Him in prayer.

If we look at the situation of the church in general throughout the world, or even a local situation or different individuals, we can see so many breaches and gaps, so much ground where the enemy can come in like a flood. How very much God is looking for intercessors! "He wondered that there was no intercessor." God can never be surprised because He knows everything beforehand, but sometimes He wonders: "Why not? Why not?" More and more, I feel our corporate prayer meeting is of such a tremendous time that we need to consider it more seriously. We cannot just come and say a few prayers because God is expecting so much from this time.

May the Lord help us to be willing to give ourselves to Him for the making of intercessors.

9—All

Ephesians 6:18—Praying at all seasons, with all prayer and supplication in the Spirit, and watching unto this very thing with all perseverance and supplication for all the saints.

As you will notice in the version which I have read, the word *all* is used four times. Probably, in some of your versions, there are only three.

Prayer is not only work, it is warfare. God has a purpose, and it is to be fulfilled in His church and through His church. Because of that, the enemy is trying to fight against the purpose of God, and in doing that, the church becomes his target. That is the reason we are called to put on the whole armor of God. We do not put on any armor if there is not any warfare, but since we are exhorted to put on this armor, it implies that there is a battle. Actually, the church is engaged in spiritual warfare.

Among the complete armor which the church is to put on, we find that most of the weapons are defensive. Only two can be defensive and offensive. One is the sword of the Spirit, which is the word of God. By the word of God, you can fend off the attack of the enemy just like our Lord Jesus did when He was tempted by Satan. More than that, the sword can be used as an offensive weapon to attack.

The other weapon that is both offensive and defensive is prayer. Prayer can be defensively used to keep the enemy from attacking and also to attack the enemy and get into his territory. Of all the weapons listed here, prayer is mentioned last. As a matter of fact, it is a most strategic weapon, and it is the one that the church is called to take up and use. Because of that, the enemy tries to lull the church to sleep so as to forget to use this weapon. That is why you will find prayer becomes the most difficult of all the activities of the church. It is said that when a weak saint is on his knees, the devil trembles. That shows how effective the weapon of prayer is, and, for this reason, the enemy is afraid of it and tries to keep the saints of God from using it. I believe this is true not only today, but it has been so throughout the centuries.

We find that prayer is something that is often neglected, unused, or it is not skillfully employed. When this is so, the will of God is frustrated, delayed, postponed, and the enemy is having his time prolonged. So as we come together to pray, it is really a very important time because we want to wield this weapon that God has given to us.

In this verse, I am especially touched by the word *all*. It says "praying at all seasons," or some versions say "praying always." This really means praying at all seasons—whether it is in season or out—at every occasion and at every indication of need or trial. It does not mean that we pray at certain seasons, occasions, or times about certain things, but we are actually exhorted to pray at all seasons, on every occasion, at all times. It is a weapon which should be used all the time!

The next part of the verse reads, "With all prayer and supplication." The book Pilgrim's Progress tells us that at one time, Christian put down the sword and took up another weapon which was called "all prayer." Prayer is a weapon, just as the word of God is the sword of the Spirit, and we need to take it up. What does it mean by "all prayer"? It includes all the meanings of prayer. Sometimes prayer is communion, and sometimes it is worship. Other times it is petition, asking, interceding, believing, or proclaiming. Prayer is of all various kinds, and we need to pray with all prayer in the Spirit. In other words, it is as the Spirit leads, and sometimes, the Spirit leads us into communion, worship, petition, intercession, etc. This is all kinds of prayer.

"Watching unto this very thing with all perseverance." When we are praying, we need "all perseverance" because it is very easy to grow faint and discouraged. We must continue in prayer and watching. Prayer is like a battle. When one is in combat, he needs to be alert because the battle scene changes so often. Suddenly, the enemy attacks, and the next moment he retreats. The battle scene shifts all the time. Therefore, we must watch and discern what is going on to see if anything has changed. After the situation has changed, then we have to change our prayer. This is included in "all perseverance." It is not that we pray with our eyes closed without noticing what is going on and always praying the same prayer. The enemy may have retreated already, yet we are still praying to the front. You have to change your prayer direction because the scene has changed. It takes endurance. Sometimes, the battle is really a test of endurance. Who is able to endure to the end? The enemy tries to wear us out, but we will wear him out with "all perseverance," just like that widow wore the judge out. By the grace of God, we must persevere with all the endurance that we can find.

Finally, it says, "Supplication for all the saints." Notice it is all the saints. This battle involves all the saints. It is not just a few who are in the battle; it is the whole church. Even though many saints may not realize it, oftentimes, those who are not watchful are being attacked. If the enemy cannot attack from the front line because he finds it is pretty strong and difficult for him, then he will try to find a weak spot or weak saint, and there he will attack.

It is similar to the time when the children of Israel were in the wilderness. The enemy attacked those that lingered at the back because they did not march on as quickly as the others. Therefore, since this is how the enemy attacks, the prayer of the church has to cover all the saints, the strong and the weak. We need to reinforce those who are strong, and we must rush to help those who are weak. Thus it has to be supplication for all the saints.

This is what we have here: "at all seasons, with all prayer ... with all perseverance ... for all the saints." This is the time in which we come together and stand with God for His will to be brought into being on this earth, withstanding all the assaults of the enemy. It is an important time. And when we are in the battle, we cannot afford to sleep. We have to be awake and alert, and every brother and sister has to take up this weapon and wield it offensively and defensively. Do not let just a few pray all the time, but everyone who attends should stand in his or her place on the battlefield. Together, we can wield this strategic, all-victorious weapon called "all prayer."

10—Prayer is Work

Colossians 1:29—Whereunto also I toil, combating according to his working, which works in me in power.

Colossians 2:1-2—For I would have you know what combat I have for you, and those in Laodicea, and as many as have not seen my face in flesh; to the end that their hearts may be encouraged, being united together in love, and unto all riches of the full assurance of understanding, to the full knowledge of the mystery of God.

Colossians 4:12—Epaphras, who is one of you, the bondman of Christ Jesus, salutes you, always combating earnestly for you in prayers, to the end that ye may stand perfect and complete in all the will of God.

We mentioned before that prayer is warfare, and I would like to add something more, which is, prayer is work. Somehow, we do not consider prayer as work. We want to work for God, but in our minds, we do not consider prayer as work. Yet, it is a work in which everyone can be engaged. There are works which I cannot do; there are works which you cannot do, but the one work which we can all do is prayer. The greatest to the smallest can pray. As a matter of fact, prayer is the greatest work in the whole world. If we can see that prayer is doing God's work, then when we come together, we will work with God, and all of us can be involved.

In any work, you need strength, and prayer, especially, demands more spiritual strength than any other. It takes less strength to preach but more strength to pray. That is why we sometimes find prayer is more difficult. We feel we are so weak and do not have the strength to pray. After a day's work or a day of facing different things, we are already tired and exhausted physically and drained spiritually. Therefore, our prayer time is very difficult because it is not play, it is work. And work demands strength. Of course, the strength here is basically spiritual, but physical strength is also involved. When we are physically tired, even though our spirit is willing, our flesh is weak. We may go to sleep instead of "watching and praying," which is what the disciples did.

As we come together, we really need to wait upon the Lord as the Scripture says: "They that wait upon the Lord shall renew their strength" (Isaiah 40:31). No matter how tired we are physically or how drained we are spiritually, if we will wait upon the Lord, worship Him and look to Him, then our strength will be renewed, and we are ready to pray. We know the strength comes from the Lord. Therefore, we do not need to say we cannot pray because we are tired and weak and have lots of things on our minds. As we wait upon Him and look to Him, He will renew our strength. We will "mount up with wings as eagles," and we are able to pray.

Work also requires discipline. If we need to do some work, we must discipline ourselves because, naturally, our flesh does not want to work. There is an inertia in us. It is comfortable just to stay where we are and do nothing. It takes a little discipline for us to really break through and apply ourselves to any work, and this is true with prayer. Because we are not willing to discipline ourselves, we find we are unable to pray. We just fall back and relax, saying we do not feel like praying. We would never work if we waited until we felt like it. And if we must wait until we feel like praying, we would never pray. I suppose some of us do not pray because of this. We must discipline ourselves and break through that inertia. As we do this, we will find the more we pray, the stronger we become.

You may have heard that you do not pray if the Spirit does not move you. In other words, you have to feel a stirring in your spirit; then you open your mouth to pray. Now that is fine, but when the Spirit is not stirring you, your mind ought to help your spirit and get it stirred. If the Spirit of the Lord descends upon you and really constrains you to pray, that is good; but when your spirit does not seem to be stirred (it is not that the Holy Spirit is not stirring you; it is just that your spirit is sleeping), then you need your mind to give your spirit a little push. It is like in the old days when you would draw water, and you had to pour a little into the pump before you could draw it out. You have to prime the pump. Your mind can help your spirit. Pour a little water in, and in the beginning, it is as if you are praying with your mind, but as you continue praying, the spirit awakens and takes over. That is discipline.

Prayer is work; therefore, it requires all these things, and if we are willing to discipline ourselves, I believe everyone will find they can pray. When we come together, the one thing we want to see taking place is everyone praying. Of course, everyone is praying when we say we are praying in our hearts, but more is required than that. When we are together with brothers and sisters, and we are praying in our hearts, no one can hear us and say "amen" with us. Unless we are super-spiritual, we probably will not be able to feel people's spirits. Therefore, it does require opening our mouths and uttering what is in our hearts. When we do this, then brothers and sisters hear it and "amen" with us. This is where the prayer with one accord and the prayer of strength comes.

Our real purpose in the prayer time is not just a few praying but everyone praying. I believe this is how it should be. Do not hold back. Discipline yourself. Take a burden and enter into prayer, and as you start to pray, the burden will increase in you. It is always like that.

Paul mentioned in these verses how he toiled and labored, and that is work. He even combated. In some versions, it says "struggling or wrestling." Then it goes on: "For I would have you know what wrestling I have for you, and those in Laodicea, and as many as have not seen my face in flesh." In other words, he has never seen these people in Laodicea and Colosse. It is easy for us to pray for people whom we know because we are emotionally involved, but to pray for those we have never seen becomes very difficult. If we are truly involved with God and His purpose, then whether we have seen these people or not will not make any difference.

Paul could toil, labor, struggle, combat and wrestle because he had the heart of Christ for the people. He wanted to see God's people reach maturity, to the stature of Christ, and that urged him to pray. It was not a personal, emotional involvement but pure involvement with Christ and God's purpose. Notice it was not only Paul who was like that but Epaphras also. He labored or combated in prayer "to the end that ye may stand perfect and complete in all the will of God."

The ultimate purpose of prayer as work is that the will of God might be completed and perfected in the lives of the saints. Whether we are praying for the sick, those with problems, the people of God here and there, God's work, conferences, or world situations, the final purpose is the will of God. Everyone is called to work together with God through prayer.

Sometimes, you think, "If only I could do what this brother or sister is doing, then I would be really serving God." But all the time, there is a greater work that He has already called you to do, and you do not do it. Therefore, I do hope that each brother and sister will be encouraged and realize that we do not come together to play or watch. We come to work! I hope everyone will join in the work. Otherwise, a few will have to work all the time while the rest just sit and watch. That is not fair. We must join together in the work just like you find in the book of Acts where the 120 gave themselves to continual prayer with one accord. As you read on, you see that when the two apostles were released and came to their own company, the whole company raised their voices and prayed. It was everyone. That is how the work should be. You do not want your brothers and sisters to work themselves to death while you are just loitering around. That is unkind.

Also, there is a reward. When the prayers are answered, that is our reward. I encourage brothers and sisters as we come together that we learn. Ultimately, I think the church is not really manifested or expressed until everyone is functioning. When this happens, we see a healthy body. If only part of the body is functioning, it is a sick body, and it is like dragging and dragging a half-paralyzed body. The Lord wants us to be healthy; that is why we all need to work.

11—House of Prayer

II Chronicles 6:18-21—But will God indeed dwell with man on the earth? behold, the heavens and the heaven of heavens cannot contain thee; how much less this house which I have built! Yet have respect unto the prayer of thy servant, and to his supplication, Jehovah, my God, to hearken unto the cry and to the prayer which thy servant prayeth before thee; that thine eyes may be open upon this house day and night, upon the place in which thou hast said thou wouldest put thy name: to hearken unto the prayer which thy servant prayeth toward this place. And hearken unto the supplications of thy servant, and of thy people Israel, which they shall pray toward this place, and hear thou from thy dwelling-place, from the heavens, and when thou hearest, forgive.

II Chronicles 6:40-42—Now, my God, I beseech thee, let thine eyes be open and let thine ears be attentive unto the prayer that is made in this place. And now, arise, Jehovah Elohim, into thy resting-place, thou and the ark of thy strength: let thy priests, Jehovah Elohim, be clothed with salvation, and let thy saints rejoice in thy goodness. Jehovah Elohim, turn not away the face of thine anointed: remember mercies to David thy servant.

Matthew 21:13—And he says to them, It is written, My house shall be called a house of prayer.

Solomon built the temple, and when it was dedicated, he acknowledged that God really did not dwell in a physical house because even "the heavens and the heaven of heavens cannot contain thee; how much less this house which I have built!" Even though it was a magnificent building, he understood that God did not actually dwell there; yet, it was where God put His name. Because His name was there, Solomon expected God to hear all the prayers that would be offered in the temple and even those prayers that were offered towards it.

In II Chronicles 6, Solomon raised up all kinds of imaginable situations such as being attacked by the enemy, famine, war, pestilence, plagues, people sinning, or taking an oath. He said whatever the situation might be—whether the people there repented and prayed in the temple, or if they had been taken to the corners of the earth and prayed towards the temple—God would hear, forgive, deliver, and answer.

When our Lord Jesus was on earth, He said, "My house shall be called a house of prayer." So the temple was actually a house of prayer for all nations. It was not only for the children of Israel, but even if strangers should turn towards the temple and pray, God would hear. Can you imagine the temple standing there and no prayers being offered in it or towards it? It is impossible.

Under the New Covenant, we are the temple of God. In Ephesians 2, it is stated very clearly: "Being built upon the foundation of the apostles and prophets, Jesus Christ himself being the corner-stone, in whom all the building fitted together increases to a holy temple in the Lord; in whom ye also are built together for a habitation of God in the Spirit" (vv. 20-22). Today the Lord is building a temple with living stones. He is building us together to be the house of God, and in this house, you will find not only His name but also His presence. In Matthew 18, He said, "For where two or three are gathered together unto my name, there am I in the midst of them" (v. 20). Today, God is actually dwelling in this house. He did not do that with the temple built by Solomon, but He does dwell in this temple built with living stones. He said, "There am I in the midst of them." He makes His residence in the church. Therefore, today, how much more real is the church as the house of prayer for all nations.

The church is called to pray, and we will find this was true at the beginning of church history, as recorded in the book of Acts.

"And they persevered in the teaching and fellowship of the apostles, in breaking of bread and prayers" (Acts 2:42).

Whenever anything has happened, the church has turned to prayer. It is a praying church; it is a house of prayer. The ministry of the church is basically prayer, but unfortunately, today people seem to flock to the time when the word is ministered. Thank God for that. People love to hear the Word, but when it comes to the time of prayer, many people disappear. And in some places, there is no prayer meeting because people will not come to pray. If that is the case, it shows whether there is a church or not. If there is a church, there should be prayer. Unless we come to an understanding of what prayer is, we do not know what the church is. Or, to put it in another way, we never really enter into the life of the church. It is a very serious thing to come to a meeting of prayer. If we do not see the importance of coming together to pray, then actually, we do not know what the church is, and we do not practice church life. People who come together to pray are those who are really appreciating, appropriating, and living church life.

In the Old Testament, when the priests served in the temple offering incense at the golden altar of incense, this was the highest service they could ever perform. We are told that at the time of Christ, a lot could fall upon a certain priest to offer incense at the golden altar of incense. He could do this only once in his lifetime. It could never be repeated. Many priests served during their entire lives in the temple and were never given this privilege by God. Today we are not only the house of God; we are also the priesthood serving in the house of God. Everyone has the privilege to burn incense at the golden altar of incense—not just once, but it is a lifetime job. We can do it all the time.

Furthermore, in the Old Testament times, when the priests burned incense, there was a veil separating the altar of incense from the mercy seat; but today, the veil is rent. When we pray, we enter into the very presence of God with unveiled face—face to face. There we can offer prayers on behalf of God's people, for the world, for God's interest, His kingdom, and His concern. Every imaginable situation can be brought before the Lord in prayer. That is our calling, our privilege, and our right. I do hope we appreciate this.

Suppose we were living thousands of years ago as priests in the temple built by Solomon or rebuilt by the remnant. We would long to burn incense at the golden altar of incense, but more than likely, we would not have the opportunity. However, in our day, it is a privilege and a right that is ours.

Can you even imagine that we are not exercising our right and appreciating our privilege to burn incense at the golden altar of incense?

If we could only know what this means, we would appreciate the time when the church gathers together to pray. We know that when we pray, He is listening; His eyes are open; His ears are open; His heart is open; His name is here; His presence is here. How much He will forgive, deliver, and answer. May we appreciate this time when we come together.

12—Prayer and Humility

II Chronicles 7:14—And my people, who are called by my name, humble themselves, and pray, and seek my face, and turn from their wicked ways; then will I hear from the heavens, and forgive their sin, and heal their land.

I wonder how much we relate humility with prayer. I suppose when we think of prayer, we think of faith, confidence, and boldness. Very rarely do we think of humility. We know that faith is essential because without faith, our prayer will not be answered. If we believe that whatsoever we ask we receive, we shall receive it. Faith is essential; but also, we need confidence. "We are confident that if we ask him anything according to his will he hears us" (I John 5:14). We need boldness. We enter into the Holy of Holies with boldness. We need all these things—faith, confidence, and boldness.

What is faith? Faith is not something we can manufacture. It does not have its source in us. It is looking off unto Jesus. If we look at ourselves, we will have no faith. But if we forget about ourselves and look at the Lord Jesus, then faith rises up within us, and that is humility.

We need confidence. When we come to pray, we need to be confident that He hears us. But what is confidence? We have no confidence in the flesh; our confidence is in God, and that is humility.

We also need boldness. We have no boldness in ourselves because we have no merits upon which we can approach God. We have boldness because of the blood of the Lamb, and that again is humility.

Therefore, when you think of real prayer, it is actually based on humility. If we are proud of ourselves and have confidence and boldness in ourselves, that is presumption. We have no right nor merit. There is nothing with which we can force God to hear our prayer. Therefore, as we come to pray, we need to humble ourselves before Him. Humility is the only attitude that we must have when we come to pray.

Remember the parable the Lord Jesus told about the Pharisee and the publican (see Luke 18:9-14). The Pharisee entered into the temple to pray with what seemed to be boldness and much faith—but in himself—not in God. He was very confident, but he was not heard. The publican, who was a tax collector, not only had no boldness or confidence in himself, but he had no faith. He cried out: "Lord, be merciful to me, a sinner." He knew that there was nothing in himself with which he could approach God; it was all in God. That is humility. Since he was humble, he was heard. When we come to pray, we need this attitude of humility, having no dependence on ourselves. We are not to come as if we have faith. If we think we have faith, we do not.

In Mark 9, we read about the father who came to the Lord Jesus and said, "If thou couldst do anything, be moved with pity on us, and help us" (v. 22b). The Lord replied, "The if thou couldst is if thou couldst believe" (v. 23). That is the issue. It is not whether the Lord can or cannot but whether you can believe or not. Remember the father who cried out: "I believe, help mine unbelief" (v. 24b). Now that is faith. So far as the father was concerned, there was unbelief; but he wanted to believe and looked to the Lord to help his unbelief.

As we come together to pray, we come as nothing. Do not think that because you have had a good day, therefore, you will have faith that the Lord will hear you. Or do not think because you have done the right thing, you will have boldness to come to God. Do not think there is anything in you that deserves His hearing your prayer. On the contrary, we have to come with deep humility. There is absolutely nothing in us. We have no right, and we do not deserve anything. It is all up to Him. And with that kind of attitude, when we come to pray, we find that He hears us because God gives grace to the humble and resists the proud.

"And my people, who are called by my name, humble themselves, and pray." We are His people; we are called by His name. As a matter of fact, we have gathered together in His name; but what does the Lord require of us? He asks that we humble ourselves and pray. That is the attitude we must have.

"And seek my face." That is what prayer really is. Prayer is not just presenting things to Him which we would like. It is seeking His face. We may have a problem, and we do not know how it can be solved, but if we see Him, the problem will be solved. Oftentimes, people pray as if they are twisting God's arm. That is not prayer. Prayer is seeking God's face, but we will not be able to do that if we are not humble. Seeking God's face means seeking to know His will and His mind, and when we see His face, everything is open and clear. It is not a matter of reasonings; it is not a matter of pros and cons; it is seeing His face. If we see His face, then everything is settled.

"And turn from their wicked ways." If we see His face, I believe the natural result will be the realization that our ways have not been good, even that they are wicked, and we need to turn from them. We have not been walking as we should.

"But if we walk in the light as he is in the light, we have fellowship with one another, and the blood of Jesus Christ his Son cleanses us from all sin" (I John 1:7)"

With the light of His countenance shining upon us, it will remove all our wickedness, all our sins, all our unrighteousness, all our shadows, and shades. In other words, we will be in union and communion with the Lord. It is then that the Lord will say, "Then will I hear from the heavens, and forgive their sin, and heal their land." God says He will not only hear, but He will forgive and also heal.

In this verse, we see the absolute necessity of humility when we come to pray. Let us truly humble ourselves before the Lord, seek His face, turn from our wicked ways, and He will hear, forgive and heal. This is in no way contradictory to faith, confidence, and boldness. We need faith, yes, but faith is looking off unto Jesus, which is humility. We do not believe in ourselves; we believe in Him. In a sense, it humbles us because we like to believe in ourselves, thinking we can do it. We like to feel confident, but it is in true humility that we have real faith, real confidence, and real boldness. It is not a contradiction. It is actually humility that leads us to faith, confidence, and boldness.

13—Continual Prayer

Acts 1:14—These gave themselves all with one accord to continual prayer, with several women, and Mary the mother of Jesus, and with his brethren.

I Corinthians 15:6 tells us that on one occasion, the Lord Jesus appeared to five hundred brethren after He was raised from the dead. We do not know if that happened when He was taken up or not, but very likely it was. So actually, five hundred brethren saw the Lord and no doubt heard what He told them: "... not to depart from Jerusalem, but to await the promise of the Father." "But ye will receive power, the Holy Spirit having come upon you, and ye shall be my witnesses both in Jerusalem, and in all Judea and Samaria, and to the end of the earth" (Acts 1:4, 8).

In the first chapter of Acts, after the ascension of the Lord, only one hundred and twenty believers returned to Jerusalem and gathered in that upper chamber to give themselves with one accord to continual prayer. Five hundred brethren saw and heard Him, but only one hundred and twenty acted on what He said. They went back to Jerusalem to wait for the promise of the Holy Spirit. However, they did not wait passively but gave themselves actively to continual prayer until the promise came on the day of Pentecost.

Oftentimes, we think if we have God's promise, we do not need to give ourselves to continual prayer. If we continue to pray, will it not be an indication that we do not have faith? No, this is not true. The truth is that since we have the promise, we give ourselves to continual prayer so the promise might be fulfilled. These believers gave themselves to continual prayer. They prayed and prayed and prayed for ten days. They prayed the same prayer with one accord—that is, they prayed with one mind for the promise to be fulfilled.

I think it is important for us at this juncture, especially in view of the conference which is coming within the month, to believe that He who has originated this conference will bless it. We cannot afford to sit back and be passive. If we do, we may not receive the promise. I wonder what happened to the three hundred and eighty people who had the promise yet did not return to Jerusalem. Maybe they returned home and were passively waiting for the promise to come to them, but when Pentecost came, they were not there. That should encourage those of us who have His promise to give ourselves to continual prayer. We need to pray and pray. We should not feel it is monotonous to do this or tire of it or even think that by praying too much, we do not have faith in Him. It is the opposite that is true. It is because we believe His promise; therefore, we pray and pray that His promise might be fulfilled.

Even though we might go over the same thing, even praying the same thing, yet it can be living and real and not necessarily vain repetition. The Bible does not forbid us to repeat; it only tells us not to have vain repetition. Vain repetition simply means you repeat something, but your heart is not in it. You might repeat something because you have a wrong concept, thinking that if you pray long enough, then God will hear, but if your prayer is too short, God will probably miss it. That is vain repetition. But we may repeat and repeat and repeat. Even our Lord Jesus repeated three times in the garden of Gethsemane. In II Corinthians 12,

Paul repeated three times. And Elijah repeated seven times. So it is not a matter of repetition; it is vain repetition. If our heart is in what we repeat, it reinforces, strengthens, and builds.

We can compare prayer to a balance. One prayer is like adding one weight, and when you have added enough weight to the balance, it will begin to tilt. Sometimes, we stop before there is enough prayer and it goes unanswered. Therefore, we just need to continue to pray. It is not that we should only pray when we are together, but we need to give ourselves to continual prayer.

What does it mean to give ourselves to continual prayer? If you give yourself to do something, you do not do that thing once a week; you continue doing it all the time. So in view of the upcoming conference, we should be occupying ourselves with continual prayer throughout this month. If we expect— and we do—that the promise and the blessing of the Lord will come upon His people at the conference, then we need to give ourselves to continual prayer. We have not yet prayed sufficiently for this conference.

If we who are here can really give ourselves with one accord to continual prayer, then our experience will be as the day of Pentecost. When they were praying in that upper chamber, there was one thing on their mind—the promise of the Father. Evidently, they just concentrated their prayer on this one thing, and they prayed for ten days. During those ten days, something happened. In the first chapter of Acts, we read about Peter sharing with those gathered in the upper room concerning a vacancy in the apostleship as a result of Judas hanging himself (see vv. 15-26). It was necessary for it to be filled in preparation for the day when the Holy Spirit would come. I believe this will happen to us also as we set our hearts to pray for the conference. No doubt the Holy Spirit will show us where there are loopholes, gaps, and vacancies that need to be filled. This is all done as a preparation that when the Holy Spirit comes, everything will be ready for Him. I believe the time within this last month before the conference is very critical. It is not simply praying and praying, but I feel the Lord desires to do some adjusting with us individually and corporately. We should be open to it and ready for it, and I believe the promise will then come.

14—Prayer with One Accord

Acts 4:23-31—And having been let go, they came to their own company, and reported all that the chief priests and elders had said to them. And they, having heard it, lifted up their voice with one accord to God, and said, Lord, thou art the God who made the heaven and the earth and the sea, and all that is in them; who hast said by the mouth of thy servant David, Why have the nations raged haughtily and the peoples meditated vain things? The kings of the earth were there, and the rulers were gathered together against the Lord and against his Christ. For in truth against thy holy servant Jesus, whom thou hadst anointed, both Herod and Pontius Pilate, with the nations, and peoples of Israel, have been gathered together in this city to do whatever thy hand and thy counsel had determined before should come to pass. And now, Lord, look upon their threatenings, and give to thy bondmen with all boldness to speak thy word, in that thou stretchest out thy hand to heal, and that signs and wonders take place through the name of thy holy servant Jesus. And when they had prayed, the place in which they were assembled shook, and they were all filled with the Holy Spirit, and spoke the word of God with boldness.

This passage, which is on corporate prayer, is one of the most wonderful in the Scriptures. Peter and John had just been threatened by the council not to speak in the name of the Lord Jesus. After their release, they came to their own and reported what had happened, and then the Scripture says, "And they, having heard it, lifted up their voice with one accord to God, and said ..." Now we know that there were already in Jerusalem at that time thousands of believers because on the day of Pentecost, aside from the one hundred and twenty believers, there were now three thousand. Before this incident, more were added as you can see in the preceding verse: "But many of those who had heard the word believed; and the number of the men had become about five thousand" (Acts 4:4). This means that there were thousands of believers there, and they lifted up their voice with one accord to God. It was not a few, not even a hundred, but thousands who lifted up their voice with one accord and prayed.

There are many places in the Scripture where prayers are recorded, but most of them are prayed by one person. For instance, Paul prayed, and his prayers are recorded. Daniel prayed, and his prayer is recorded. But in this instance, the Holy Spirit records the prayer of the church. Thousands of people were praying, and they prayed in such a manner that the Holy Spirit was able to record their prayer because they prayed as one man. It was not the prayer of one person. Now, if one person was praying, probably, it would be comparatively easy to pray in this manner. But thousands were praying, and the Holy Spirit recorded their prayer as if only one man was praying—and it was.

As you read the record of their prayer, you will see a divine order. It was a perfect prayer and one that was not organized beforehand. First of all, they declared that God is the God of heaven, the earth, and the sea. Then they quoted the Old Testament Scripture and found it was fulfilled in the life of our Lord Jesus. This formed the basis of their prayer. Next, they mentioned the events that had happened. Then they asked God to give them boldness to speak. It was as if only one man prayed. There was no discord or division. Even though we are few in number, can the Holy Spirit record our prayer in this manner? Or will it be that one will pray for this and another pray for that? If it is not the Holy Spirit who is in charge, then who can do such a thing? These people were so given to the Lord that the Holy Spirit was able to pray through them in such a manner that there was perfect order.

Take note that they lifted up their voice, and in the original *voice* is singular. Some versions render the word voices, but I like the singular. They lifted up their voice—only one voice—so many people but only one voice. I do not think that on this occasion, thousands of people lifted up their voices and prayed. Now, this is done sometimes. As a matter of fact, I was brought up under that kind of praying because I was saved among the Holiness people where we all prayed together, and no one hears anyone. I do not believe this was what happened there because they lifted up their voice—only one voice—and that one voice was carried by many people. It was not Peter who was praying; it was not John who represented the whole company and prayed. No. They lifted up their voice with one accord. Therefore, it must have been that the Holy Spirit touched upon many different people, and in all their prayers, there was an order, and it came out a perfect prayer. That is corporate prayer, and this is the first recorded corporate prayer of the church. This is a marvelous passage if we know and consider the background.

When the Holy Spirit is truly in charge (and He should be and He is because the Lord said where two or three are gathered together, there am I in the midst), representing the Head, He is directing the body to pray. Whoever is being used by the Holy Spirit at that moment is not just praying his own prayers; he is praying the prayer of the Head. When this happens, there will be harmony with no jarring notes. Then the Holy Spirit is able to record it. If everyone just prays his own prayer, how will the Holy Spirit record it? If He should record John's prayer, it would not be Peter's prayer; but here, the Holy Spirit is able to record it as the prayer of the whole church. It is a tremendous thing, and I sincerely believe that when the Holy Spirit is in charge, and we are submitted to Him, this will happen.

Unfortunately, we do not always submit ourselves to the Holy Spirit; that is, when the Holy Spirit touches upon a certain brother or sister, they refuse to cooperate. Or sometimes the Holy Spirit has not touched upon a person, and he starts to pray. But here in Acts, the whole company was yielded and available. When we come together to pray, are we available to the Holy Spirit, or have we decided that we are going to pray or not going to pray? Do we allow the Holy Spirit to actually pray through us? If we do, then we will find it is truly marvelous, just as it was with the church in the time of Acts.

Here in Acts, we find the church was challenged—and not just Peter and John. They were threatened, but this challenge was against the whole church, and they took it up. How did they do it? It was not by matching the world with their own cleverness or by fighting against the world with their own power; it was by turning to God in prayer. Prayer is the weapon of the church. This is the way we meet every challenge, whether it is a threat or something else. We know the church is always being challenged, both negatively and positively, and when this happens, the only recourse we have is to pray as a church. The church should take up any challenge with prayer—not with discussion, negotiation, or confrontation.

As the church in Acts prayed, they had absolutely no idea of retreating. On the contrary, they asked the Lord to give them boldness to speak. The council had told them to shut their mouths, but because the church had been given a mandate from the Lord that they "shall be my witnesses both in Jerusalem, and in all Judea and Samaria, and to the end of the earth" (Acts 1:8), they asked for boldness to speak in the name of the Lord Jesus. The result was that the place literally shook, and they were all filled with the Holy Spirit and spoke the word of God with boldness. It was not just a few, but all were filled because they prayed with one accord. Boldness was not just given to the apostles but to all. That was the way in which God answered their prayer.

As we come together, I feel that there are many challenges before us. The one which I think is evident is the conference. It is a challenge to the whole church and not just a few. We really need to take up that challenge and pray that the Lord will enable us to stand, withstand and to utter His word, His will, and accomplish His work for this conference. There is a conflict in this because the enemy is trying to shut us up, but we have a mandate from heaven, and we must ask the Lord to give us boldness to accomplish His purpose. Because we do have this challenge, we need to lift up our voice with one accord to God; and if we do, we will all be filled with the Holy Spirit. People who do not take up the challenge and pray miss the blessing. We must continue to pray and meet this challenge that His name may be exalted.

15—Unceasing Prayer

Acts 12:5—Peter therefore was kept in the prison; but unceasing prayer was made by the assembly to God concerning him.

Acts 12:11-16—And Peter, being come to himself, said, Now I know certainly that the Lord has sent forth his angel and has taken me out of the hand of Herod and all the expectation of the people of the Jews. And having become clearly conscious in himself, he came to the house of Mary, the mother of John who was surnamed Mark, where were many gathered together and praying. And when he had knocked at the door of the entry, a maid came to listen, by name Rhoda; and having recognised the voice of Peter, through joy did not open the entry, but running in, reported that Peter was standing before the entry. And they said to her, Thou art mad. But she maintained that it was so. And they said, It is his angel. But Peter continued knocking: and having opened, they saw him and were astonished.

This incident happened when the gospel seemed to spread and prosper. It had spread not only in Jerusalem but through Judea into Samaria and even to Antioch. During this time, Saul, the archenemy of the church, was converted. So in a sense, it was at a time when the church seemed to grow and prosper and be victorious. Then the enemy struck. Herod beheaded James and had Peter seized and put in prison.

When God is working, the enemy is also busy. Peter was taken before the Passover, which was probably the next day. Therefore, Peter was kept in prison through the Feast of Unleavened Bread, which continued for seven days. Herod's idea was to release Peter from prison after the Feast of Unleavened Bread and have him killed. So Peter was actually kept in prison for at least eight days. The Bible says: "Peter therefore was kept in prison."

It seemed as if the enemy was able to do what he wanted without restraint. For eight days, Peter was kept in prison, "but unceasing prayer was made by the assembly to God concerning him." I like the word *but* and you need to put it in the right place. We often say, "Everything is fine, but ..." That is the wrong place. Peter was kept in prison, but unceasing prayer was made by the church. Now that is the right place. This was a difficult situation for the church at that time— James, the brother of John, had been killed, and Peter was kept in prison. Nevertheless, there was one thing the church could do, and that was to pray. The weapon which the church has is unceasing prayer. This is the way the church always meets a crisis. Of course, the power of prayer is not in prayer itself; it is in God to whom we pray. In other words, prayer links the church with God, and He is the Almighty God!

God could have delivered Peter on the first night, but He did not. He allowed him to be kept there until the very last night before he would have been released, judged, and killed, but our God is never in a hurry, and He is never late. Probably, the reason for this was so the church might continue to pray. They just kept on praying as long as Peter was in prison. We do not know how they prayed. Did they pray and ask God to free Peter? James had been beheaded, and I certainly do not think it was wrong for them to pray that God would spare Peter. The church really did not know what God's will was—whether He would release Peter or whether he would be killed like James. That was why it was such a shock to Peter when he was released.

In Acts 4, when Peter and John were released, they came to their own, lifted up their voice, and there was no uncertainty in their prayer. They knew what God's will was, and they had a mandate from heaven. They did not ask the Lord whether they should be quiet or continue to preach in the name of the Lord. No, they just asked God to give them boldness to speak in the name of the Lord. Their prayer was so certain, so positive and sure, with no hesitation. They asked God for the thing which they felt should be asked, and their prayer was answered.

In chapter 12, we find an entirely different situation. They kept on praying but never knew exactly what God would do. Otherwise, you cannot explain how they reacted when God answered their prayer. And when He did answer, they did not even know that was the way. It showed that they really did not know what the will of God was. Most likely, when they prayed, they asked that the Lord's will might be done. Of course, they wanted the Lord to spare Peter; yet they were resigned to whatever the will of God would be.

Sometimes, people think that if we say in our prayer, "Lord, if it is in Your will ..." or "Your will be done ..." it is an indication that we have no faith. Some of the time, that is true, but not always. Many times, when people do not know the will of God, they become very presumptuous and think they must tell God what to do. They have to believe this is so, and to them, this is faith. However, this is not necessarily

83

faith. If you have the word of God, then you can pray positively, and that is faith. But when you do not know the will of God, and you are praying unceasingly for the Lord to do whatever He feels is right, resigning yourself to His will, this is not an indication of lack of faith. Sometimes, we think if we are resigned to the will of God, then we do not need to pray. We just become passive and wait for God's will to come to pass, but this is the wrong attitude. We need to be resigned to the will of God, but we also need to pray unceasingly that His will may be manifested. To pray that God's will be done is not an indication that we do not have faith. On the contrary, it shows that we are resigned to His will. What attitude pleases the Lord more than resignation to His will? God certainly knows what is best, and He knows what to do.

Here we find that the church was not clear as to what God would do, yet they prayed unceasingly with the spirit of resignation, and God answered their prayer. You would think that Peter—who had been in prison for eight days, knowing he would be taken out the next day with the expectation that the Jews would have him killed—would not have been able to sleep that last night. Of course, God could have delivered him on the first day or on any of the following days, but that did not happen. And it seemed that God was not going to deliver him. Peter went to sleep—a deep sleep. How could he do that? He resigned himself to God's will. That is faith. He did not agitate or agonize but rested in faith. He was prepared for God's will, whatever it might be. He was sleeping, but the church was praying. If the church had been sleeping, then something would have been wrong. The person who is really involved should sleep, and that is faith; but the church that stands with him should pray, and that is faith. So if any brother or sister has a problem and they are agitated, then it is a lack of faith. They should learn to rest, believing that God's will will be done—and leave the church to pray for them. I do believe that we are here to pray in order that our brothers and sisters who have problems may go to sleep, and God's will will be done.

They really prayed because after Peter was released, he did not realize it was true. He did not expect it. He thought it was a dream, but when he realized it was true, he had to think twice before he knew where to go. Why is this so? There were so many homes where prayer meetings were going on, and he just went to one of them. The Bible said many were praying in that home—not a few. And they probably prayed until the morning light, at least until after midnight, I would think. They did not give up even when they did not know what God would do. They did believe He would do whatever was His will, and they stood with God until it was manifested one way or the other.

Sometimes, I really feel that we have this kind of concept: When we pray, we have to be very definite and positive, telling God what He must do, and that is faith. If you cannot do this and you pray "Thy will be done," then you do not have faith, and your prayer will not be answered. I believe we have to be open to either way. Should the Lord give us His word and we still say, "If it is Thy will," then we doubt God's will. It is a lack of faith. But when we do not have this word from the Lord and do not know His will, then it is not wrong to pray "Thy will be done" with the spirit of resignation. I believe this spirit of resignation really pleases the Lord. Oftentimes, people think that having that kind of spirit means your prayers are not answered. On the contrary, that is the kind of spirit that God loves. It is not a passive spirit but an active spirit wanting God's will to be done, resigning ourselves to it, standing for it, and praying until it is manifested. That is faith!

I believe this instance may help some because we do have various situations where we have the word of God, yet in others, we do not. Therefore, how do you pray when you do not have the definite word of God? You can still pray, and you should pray with faith in the will of God, that His will is a perfect will and whatever it will be is best.

May the Lord help us as we continue to pray.

16—The Song of Triumph

II Chronicles 20:20-23—And they rose early in the morning, and went forth towards the wilderness of Tekoa; and as they went forth, Jehoshaphat stood and said, Hear me, Judah, and ye inhabitants of Jerusalem! Believe in Jehovah your God, and ye shall be established; believe his prophets, and ye shall prosper! And he consulted with the people, and appointed singers to Jehovah, and those that should praise in holy splendour, as they went forth before the armed men, and say, Give thanks to Jehovah; for his lovingkindness [endureth] forever! And when they began the song of triumph and praise, Jehovah set liers-in-wait against the children of Ammon, Moab, and mount Seir, who had come against Judah, and they were smitten. And the children of Ammon and Moab stood up against the inhabitants of Mount Seir, to exterminate and destroy [them]; and when they had made an end of the inhabitants of Seir, they helped to destroy one another.

This is a most wonderful and unusual story that we find in the history of the children of Judah. A great multitude from Ammon, Moab, and Mount Seir had come against the little kingdom of Judah, but they were destroyed. When Jehoshaphat, who was the king at that time, heard that this great army was coming he was afraid, and he had every right to be because Israel was such a small country. They had no way to fight against their enemy, but Jehoshaphat set his heart towards the Lord. First, he proclaimed a fast; then he gathered the children of Judah together and prayed, "For we have no might in the presence of this great company which cometh against us, neither know we what to do; but our eyes are upon thee" (I Chronicles 20:12b). After that prayer, the Spirit of God came upon Jahaziel, and he said: "Fear not, nor be dismayed by reason of this great multitude; for the battle is not yours, but God's. Tomorrow go down against them (20:15b-16a). "Ye shall not have to fight on this occasion: set yourselves, stand and see the salvation of Jehovah who is with you!" (20:17a).

The next morning they rose early. They went forth, and as they did, Jehoshaphat consulted with the people. He encouraged them and said, "Believe in Jehovah your God, and ye shall be established" (20:20b). They had such faith in God that they appointed singers to the Lord who were clothed in holy splendor, and they marched before the army. Never before was there such a scene. "And when they began the song of triumph and praise, Jehovah set liers-in-wait against the children of Ammon, Moab, and Mount Seir" (20:22). The enemies helped destroy one another. It was a great victory!

This passage came to me two days ago. This will be our last prayer time before the conference, and as it draws nearer and nearer, probably, we will begin to feel the pressure upon us. There are many needs that must be met. We do thank God that most have been met already, but there are still more. We know that if the Lord is working, the enemy is busy. So far as we are concerned, we have every reason to be afraid. When the conference is one year away, we have boldness, but when it is right at the door, we begin to tremble. It is not only in the length of time but in what is behind the scene. How can we undertake such a big thing? A spiritual battle is raging, and it gets fiercer and fiercer as the time draws near. Now the only thing we can do is set our face toward the Lord. We will acknowledge, as Jehoshaphat did, that we have no might and we do not even know what to do, but our eyes are upon the Lord. If our eyes are upon the Lord, we will see that the battle is His, not ours.

It is true, we have to have our weapons shined and ready. We have to set ourselves and march to the battlefield, but we are not to fight. The Lord will fight for us. It is His battle. If we believe in the Lord, we will be established. Now, do we believe in the Lord? Do we believe that this battle is truly His? If the battle is His, He has already overcome. Two thousand years ago, on Calvary's cross, He crushed the enemy's head. The victory is already there, and we are to go forth to see that victory.

As far as the regular order is concerned, first, we pray, and then we praise. If we pray and have faith, even before we see the answer or have received the answer, we can start to praise. We do not need to wait until everything is finished and then praise. We can praise by faith. This is almost like what we find in Mark 11:24 when the Lord said, "Whatsoever ye pray for and ask, believe that ye receive it." First, we receive it in faith, and then it will come to pass for us; we will receive it in fact. Do we have such faith in our God? Do we need to wait until we see the fact before we can start to praise? Or do we have such faith in Him, knowing that Calvary gives us such assurance because the battle is His? He has already won. Therefore, we can praise Him beforehand.

I believe this is what God wants us to do. This is the time that we should set singers in holy splendor. It is the time that the singers should march before the army. Of course, it does not mean that the army should not go forth. The army has to go forth with their weapons shined and ready, but they are not to fight. The Lord fights for us. Now, this praise before the fact is not only a sign of faith, but it speeds the victory because the Bible says that when they began the song of triumph and praise, God started to work. So I do believe that we still need to pray—the army has to go forth—but let us have the singers go before the army.

Also, let us not forget that after the victory was won and they plundered the enemy for three days, they entered the valley of Berachah. There they gave thanks and blessed the Lord. After the victory is won, we have to go to the valley. We have to humble ourselves and bless the Lord because it is not by our might nor by our power; it is by His Spirit that this is done. Therefore, may the Lord encourage us as we continue to pray, and we begin by praising.

17—Watering the Seed With Prayer

II Thessalonians 1:3, 11—We ought to thank God always for you, brethren, even as it is meet, because your faith increases exceedingly, and the love of each one of you all towards one another abounds. ... To which end we also pray always for you, that our God may count you worthy of the calling, and fulfill all the good pleasure of his goodness and the work of faith with power.

In verse 3, we find the apostle Paul, with Silvanus and Timotheus, thanking God always for the Thessalonian believers. They thanked God because the faith of the believers increased and their love for one another abounded. Then verse 11 says, "We also pray always for you." Oftentimes, we think that prayer precedes thanks. We thank God because our prayer is answered, and I think this is right. Whenever we pray, and our prayer is answered, it is the time that we should give thanks unto the Lord. It would be very wrong if we were to just go away and never return to give our thanks to Him, as we find in the Gospels when the Lord healed the ten lepers. The nine felt fine and went their way. Only one, a Samaritan, came back to give thanks to the Lord. The Lord asked where the other nine were. If we have prayed concerning anything and our prayer is answered, we should never forget to return and thank the Lord. If we do forget, it shows how ungrateful we are after we have received what we asked of Him.

It is true that thanks to the Lord follows prayer, but in this chapter, we find thanksgiving first. After the apostles have given thanks to the Lord for what He has done with these believers, then they continue on with prayer. We think that after we have given thanks, then the case is closed; there is no more to be done. But after we have given thanks, then we should begin to pray again because there is no limit to what God can and will do. We have prayed, and He has answered. But if we do not continue on with further prayer, we are limiting God. As we see that He has answered our prayer, it encourages us to pray more in order that the Lord may be able to work and do more.

After the apostle Paul and his companions had thanked the Lord for what they had seen in the Thessalonian believers, they continued to pray, saying, "that our God may count you worthy of the calling, and fulfill all the good pleasure of his goodness and the work of faith with power." When we first pray, and our prayer is answered, it is like a seed that is sown and falls into the ground. Then we give thanks and continue to pray. This is to water the seed that it may grow and give increase.

At this time, we want to give thanks to the Lord for answered prayer during the conference—to say the least, the weather. The Lord marvelously answered prayer in so many things. Some we have already noticed, and many we do not even know. Therefore, it is but right for us to return thanks; but after we have done this, do we think the case is closed, or do we feel we need to continue to pray? The seed has been sown at the conference, but now it needs to be watered so that whatever the brothers and sisters, young and old, have heard, seen, or received might bring forth increase. If we do not continue with prayer, we know that we may not see much increase. That is the reason why people often say that at the conference you seem to be recharged, but after it is over, it suddenly wanes. I believe one reason for this is that before the conference, there is much prayer, but after it, we do not pray. We seem to think it is done, but it is just the beginning. Whatever the Lord has done at the conference needs to be taken up by us and watered by prayer so that there will be much increase for the Lord.

Also, there are still some loose ends that need to be tied up. How are we going to do that? We have to pray. Therefore, I do feel that we should never stop thanking the Lord for how He has marvelously and gloriously blessed us. We do not deserve all that He has done for us. This is not the time for us to just relax, sit back and be passive as if a chapter is closed and we can forget it until next year should the Lord tarry, and we have another conference. We should not commit this kind of error. We should continue to hold whatever has been done at the conference before the Lord until there is much increase for His kingdom. I believe there are things that are still not fully settled, and that is something for which we really need continued prayer. As we continue thanking the Lord, may we also receive the burden to continue to pray.

18—The Spirit Helps Our Weakness

Romans 8:26-27—And in like manner the Spirit joins also its help to our weakness; for we do not know what we should pray for as is fitting, but the Spirit itself makes intercession with groanings which cannot be uttered. But he who searches the hearts knows what is the mind of the Spirit, because he intercedes for saints according to God.

To understand these two verses, we need to keep them within their context. The preceding verses tell us how the whole creation groans, waiting for the manifestation of the sons of God, and how even we, who are the firstfruits of the Spirit, also groan in ourselves, waiting for adoption, for sonship. It is under that kind of atmosphere that we find these verses.

"And in like manner the Spirit joins also its help to our weakness." As we think of this matter of sonship—being conformed to the image of God's Son—we sense there is much infirmity and weakness in us. We find lots of things around us and even within us that are trying to pull us down, slowing our progress in the Lord and hindering us from being changed and transformed. This weakness or infirmity is a general one, and of all the weaknesses, there is one which is most evident—the weakness of prayer. When we are surrounded by our circumstances that seem to be contradictory to that for which God is calling, this is the time that we can overcome with prayer. We know we should pray and that without prayer, we cannot get through, but not only do we not know what or how to pray, sometimes, we do not even feel like praying. This is the weakest of all our weaknesses, and if it depended upon us to pray through, it would be a very, very sad thing. However, we thank God for one thing—that is, in our weakness, there is the Holy Spirit.

Sometimes, when we come to this area of prayer, we forget the Holy Spirit. It is as if we must struggle to pray the perfect prayer that will touch God's heart and change our circumstances and ourselves or move mountains. Oftentimes, we feel that we have to depend on prayer because we know we should pray. We forget that the Holy Spirit who dwells in us will come to our aid in this very area of prayer. We tend to depend upon ourselves to pray rather than the Holy Spirit. We may not be conscious of it, but we do neglect the Holy Spirit in our prayers.

Verse 26 says, "And in like manner the Spirit joins also its help to our weakness." The Holy Spirit will help us in this weakness of prayer. However, it does not mean that because there is the Holy Spirit, He will pray for us. It is true, the following words say, "The Spirit itself makes intercession with groanings which cannot be uttered ... because he intercedes for saints according to God." But the Holy Spirit will not intercede for us in the sense that He will be our substitute. He does not pray for us without our being involved. I think it is very evident that the Holy Spirit does intercede for us, but He intercedes for us in us.

He who knows the mind of God will intercede for us according to God; God is the One who searches the hearts. Verse 27 says, "But he who searches the hearts knows what is the mind of the Spirit." Our hearts and the mind of the Spirit work together. We are not praying alone, nor does the Holy Spirit intercede alone. It is the cooperation of our hearts with the mind of the Spirit. In other words, we need to have hearts before God. Our hearts must be burdened; our hearts must be open; our hearts must be willing. And as our hearts are before the Lord, the Holy Spirit who dwells in us will help us to pray according to God. If our heart is not there, we cannot expect the Holy Spirit to help us in our prayer.

In one sense, we do know what to pray in a general way because we know that we should pray for the maturity and the manifestation of the sons of God; but specifically, we do not know. In particular cases, we do not know what to pray or how to pray that which is fitting, and this is the area where the Holy Spirit will come to our aid. If our heart is not before God, nor do we care whether we grow spiritually or are transformed and conformed or have no desire for the purpose of God, then we cannot expect the Holy Spirit to help us in our prayers.

However, if we do have a heart for these things in our lives, in the church, and also in the world, and we find we do not know "the what" to pray (in the original, there is a definite article there in verse 26), this is the time when the Holy Spirit will come to our aid. He will make intercession for us according to God. When we pray, we will pray what we feel and think; but when the Holy Spirit intercedes for us, He will do so according to God because He is God, and God knows the mind of the Spirit. Sometimes it is unutterable—like a groaning which cannot be uttered—but at other times, it can be uttered. It does not mean that when the Holy Spirit comes to our aid in prayer, it is just groaning which cannot be uttered. I know in some places people take hold of this verse and try to groan, but that may be the people who are groaning and not the Holy Spirit. Now it is true that sometimes the Spirit is praying and our spirit is cooperating, but our mind does not have the understanding. Therefore, it comes out as groanings that are unutterable. But there are times when not only will our spirit respond to the Spirit, but even the mind of the Spirit will make it known to our mind, and when that is the case, we can pray intelligently. We do not need to groan. We can utter with plain words, and the effect before God is the same.

Therefore, as we come together to pray, is our heart open to the Lord? Is our heart willing? Is our heart burdened? Now, if our heart is open, willing, and burdened, we will feel our weakness, realizing we do not know exactly how or what to pray that which is fitting. It is then that we can trust the Holy Spirit to give us the direction and show us His mind. Even when we cannot understand it with our mind, our spirit can still cooperate with Him. As we look to the Holy Spirit for help, I think it will be a great encouragement to us.

Sometimes, we hesitate to pray because we do not know what or how to pray. But if we know the Holy Spirit is with us and in us, ready to give aid, we can cast ourselves upon Him; and as we cooperate with Him, He will intercede according to God. No one feels that he knows how to pray, for if he does, probably, he is praying himself. When we are really burdened before the Lord, we have to acknowledge we have a weakness. We do not know, but that should not hinder us. On the contrary, it should encourage us to pray. Therefore, let us give ourselves to the Lord and trust the Holy Spirit who is here waiting to pray in us, for us, and through us. May the Lord really help us.

19—The Incense of the Lord Jesus

Revelation 8:1-5—And when it opened the seventh seal, there was silence in the heaven about half an hour. And I saw the seven angels who stand before God, and seven trumpets were given to them. And another angel came and stood at the altar, having a golden censer; and much incense was given to him, that he might give efficacy to the prayers of all saints at the golden altar which was before the throne. And the smoke of the incense went up with the prayers of the saints, out of the hand of the angel before God. And the angel took the censer, and filled it from the fire of the altar, and cast it on the earth: and there were voices, and thunders and lightnings, and an earthquake.

Heaven was prepared to make a move, but before it could, there was silence in the heaven for half an hour. The silence was not because heaven was not going to make any move, but rather it was that heaven had to wait for something to happen before the move could be made. In other words, everything was ready in heaven, but the waiting was for something to happen on earth first. What was it? It was the prayers of the saints that heaven was waiting for, and after there was prayer on earth, then heaven answered. Immediately, there were voices, thunders, lightnings, and an earthquake. The movement began.

It is the principle of prayer that heaven must initiate. Prayer does not begin on earth; it is initiated in heaven. But after heaven initiates, it has to wait until the earth responds. Heaven discloses its will to the saints on earth because only they can know that will. After it reveals its will to the saints, there is the waiting for them to take up heaven's will and discharge it in prayer. It is then that heaven will answer and do what it has decided to do.

In reading Matthew 18:18, we think it looks as if heaven is waiting on the earth to make the first move. "Verily, I say to you, Whatsoever ye shall bind on the earth shall be bound in heaven, and whatsoever ye shall loose on the earth shall be loosed in heaven."

However, in the original, it says: "Whatsoever ye shall bind on the earth shall be having been bound in heaven, and whatsoever ye shall loose on the earth shall be having been loosed in heaven." Having been bound in heaven, it shall be on earth. And having been loosed in heaven, it shall be on earth. In other words, heaven actually initiates, and the earth takes it up in prayer, then heaven answers the prayer on earth. That is the order. I believe if we see this, we will realize the importance of the prayers of the saints. If the saints do not pray, even heaven cannot move. Whether the will of God can be done on earth depends very much upon the prayers of the saints. God is waiting. Heaven is silent for half an hour to see whether the saints will respond by offering prayers, whether there will be cooperation, sympathy, and the one mind of the saints with heaven.

After this is done, immediately, heaven will make a move. Actually, what we bind on earth has already been bound in heaven; what we loose on earth has already been loosed in heaven. However, the actual binding and loosing will not happen until we have bound and we have loosed on the basis of what heaven has bound and loosed. This is the mystery of prayer. It is a tremendous responsibility if we realize the significance of the prayers of the saints.

Sometimes, we feel overwhelmed because heaven puts such weight upon the prayers of the saints. If it did not matter to heaven whether we prayed or not or our prayers did not really carry much weight for the will of God to be done on earth as it is in heaven, then probably, we would feel like we could pray. But when we realize that heaven depends upon us to pray for its action, it is overwhelming to us. Who are we? Our prayers are so feeble and weak. Not only is there the sin of prayerlessness, but we do not know how or what to pray. Nevertheless, we know that heaven depends upon our prayers and is silent, with no movement, until we pray. So what can we do? If we do not know the importance of prayer, probably, we will dare to pray. But if we realize the significance, it causes us to ask: "How can our prayers be effectual?" This is where verse 3 comes in: "And another angel came and stood at the altar, having a golden censer; and much incense was given to him, that he might give efficacy to the prayers of all saints at the golden altar which was before the throne."

The prayers of the saints need some strengthening; therefore, much incense was added to them, which gives them efficacy. In other words, the prayers of the saints are weak and ineffectual, and the incense is given to make them effective before God.

What is this incense? In Revelation 5, the incense is the prayers of the saints, but in chapter 8:3, the incense is added to the prayers of the saints. The prayers of the saints are like incense ascending up to God, but they are too weak. Heaven cannot depend upon our weak prayers. Therefore, much

101

incense was added to give efficacy. According to the exegesis of Scripture, if the incense in chapter 5:8 refers to prayer, then the incense here in chapter 8:3 also refers to prayer. To whose prayer is it referring? It is to the prayer of our great High Priest, the Lord Jesus, who is risen and ascended and ever liveth to make intercession for us. That is much incense. He adds His prayers to ours, and that gives them efficacy. No matter how weak our prayers are, they will be answered because there is One who adds His prayers to ours. Do you remember these words of our Lord Jesus? "And Jesus lifted up his eyes on high and said, Father, I thank thee that thou hast heard me; but I knew that thou always hearest me" (John 11:41b-42a).

The prayers of our Lord Jesus are always heard, even when He was on earth. His prayers are added to ours, and that gives them the efficacy they need. So we should be encouraged that no matter how weak our prayers are, and even if we should pray wrongly, when His incense is added to them, it makes them right. On the one hand, when you realize the importance of prayer, you dare not pray; but on the other hand, you are encouraged when you see that today it is the work of our Lord as High Priest, who ever liveth to make intercession. It never ceases! He puts His prayers into ours, and when the smoke ascends, immediately, there are thunders, lightnings, and action begins.

The following story, which I shall never forget, illustrates this point. Once on a ship in a stateroom where people sat relaxing and reading, there was a grand piano. A little girl climbed to the stool and started to play, but she really didn't know how. She would just strike the notes at random, making such a terrible noise, and the people sitting there could not read. They did not know what to do. Suddenly, a man stood up and went to the piano and sat down by the girl. Whenever she would strike a note, he would strike those notes to accompany it, making beautiful music; and everybody enjoyed it. After a while, when the girl stopped playing, he stood up and said, "You should thank that girl for the good music which you have heard." Now that man was a musician.

I will always remember this story, and every time I feel my prayers are weak, I say, "Lord, accompany it and make it good." Also, every time I speak and I feel I have failed, I say, "Lord, make it good." This is our courage, our confidence, our encouragement.

Sometimes, you dare not open your mouth; but in a corporate prayer time like this, we want all the brothers and sisters to have a chance to pray and not just a few. Maybe they can pray better, that is true. Your prayer may not be as good as theirs, but the Lord knows, and He will add much incense to your prayer. Some brothers and sisters may pray very well, and the Lord may not add much incense to it; but if you do not know how to pray, the Lord will put more incense to it. Therefore, be encouraged. Even if your prayer is wrong, not too good, just a few words, and not very musical, He will make it heavenly music. When a burden is mentioned, just take it up and look to the Lord and say a word or two, and the Lord will add much incense to that, and heaven will hear.

Be encouraged!

20 — Prayer with the Spirit and the Understanding

I Corinthians 14:15-17—What is it then? I will pray with the spirit, but I will pray also with the understanding; I will sing with the spirit, but I will sing also with the understanding. Since otherwise, if thou blessest with the spirit, how shall he who fills the place of the simple Christian say Amen, at thy giving of thanks, since he does not know what thou sayest? For thou indeed givest thanks well, but the other is not edified.

We know this chapter deals with the assembly of God's people. Therefore, what is mentioned here about prayer does not refer to our personal private prayer, but it refers to the time we come together to pray—corporate prayer. It says, "I will pray with the spirit, but I will pray also with the understanding." Even though it is I who prays, yet none prays as just an individual. In other words, I will pray, and as the Spirit of God uses me as a mouthpiece to utter a prayer, I am praying as representing all the brothers and sisters. Because of this, there are two things that are essential to such prayer: I must pray with the spirit, and I must pray with the understanding.

As we gather here, we believe that the Holy Spirit is directing this time, and it is important for us to remember this. He is directing us to pray, and as He moves upon different individuals, they will respond with prayers. As the

Holy Spirit gives burden to our spirit, then we pray. To put it simply, our prayer is not just lip service; it must be from the heart. As our heart is touched by the Spirit of God, then we pour out our heart before the Lord. But since we are praying with our brothers and sisters, we must not only pray with the spirit but also with the mind, the understanding.

Sometimes, our spirit is burdened, but we do not know what or how to pray (see Romans 8:26). So the Spirit within us will groan, and it is known to God but not to the brothers and sisters who may be with us. Therefore, when we come together to pray, not only must our spirit be burdened and touched, but we must discharge our burden with plain words—words that can be understood. We understand what we are praying, and the brothers and sisters must also understand because we are praying in a representative way. We are not alone. If we are alone, we can pray with the spirit, and sometimes the groanings are unutterable. But when we are praying with brothers and sisters, we have to pray with the spirit and also with the understanding because we expect our brothers and sisters to join in with "Amen." The very fact that "Amen" is expected from the brothers and sisters proves that the one praying is praying for the whole company. As a person prays in the spirit and with understanding, then the brothers and sisters who hear will be touched by the Spirit of God, and they will respond with "Amen." In other words, when they are praying, and you understand and are touched in your spirit by the very same word that you want to utter, the very same burden that you have from the Lord, then respond with an "Amen." Don't be silent. Of course, we do not need to shout so loud that we make the prayer unheard, but we do need to respond with "Amen" to show that we are one with our brothers and sisters. Whenever your spirit is touched, and you feel that this is what you would pray if you were given the opportunity, then do not hesitate to respond with "Amen" because it will strengthen that prayer.

Of course, when we are praying, it is God to whom we are praying. We are not praying to our brothers and sisters. Sometimes, because we are so conscious of their presence, we try to put in some words for their sake. But it is a waste! Also, for the same reason, sometimes, we do not dare to utter our prayer because we are afraid that we do not have any beautiful words. It is unnecessary! As the Spirit touches us and we are burdened, we pray, and we do expect God to answer because we are praying to Him. However, if we pray with the spirit and with understanding, there is a by-product which is that our brothers and sisters will be edified. Isn't that marvelous? Sometimes, we think that only teaching or ministering of the word will edify the church; but remember, prayer will edify also. Now teaching or ministering the word is towards our brothers and sisters. It comes from God and should certainly edify and build up our brothers and sisters with the word of grace, but even though praying is unto God, yet we will find as we do so, there will be edification. In what way is this true? It is in realizing that the same Spirit of God is moving upon the hearts of His people because when you have a burden but do not have the words to discharge it, the Lord uses your brothers and sisters to utter it. Also, as you join in oneness with them in prayer, you are really built up together in love.

Prayer meetings should build up God's people. Don't go away complaining that the prayers were very poor, almost mechanical and formal. Of course, if they are mechanical and formal, they will not edify. But if we are really praying with the spirit and with understanding, they should edify each one of us. That is what the psalmist is saying in Psalm 19:14: "Let the words of my mouth and the meditation of my heart be acceptable in thy sight, O Jehovah, my rock, and my redeemer." Do not pray only with the spirit, which is the meditation of the heart, but also with the understanding, which results in the words of the mouth. Both are important.

When I was in Florida, a brother asked me this question: "When we are praying together, should I say: I pray, I ask, or should it be, we pray, we ask?" Technically, we would say *we* because we are praying together; but sometimes, you can say, I pray, I ask, remembering that you are praying in a representative way and not as an individual. You are not praying your private individual prayer; you are praying on behalf of all the brothers and sisters.

May the Lord help us when we pray together!

21—Praying in the Holy Spirit

Jude 20-21—But ye, beloved, building yourselves up on your most holy faith, praying in the Holy Spirit, keep yourselves in the love of God, awaiting the mercy of our Lord Jesus Christ unto eternal life.

These two verses give the positive aspect of those who are beloved of the Lord. The passage which is right before this gives all the negative things, but here, Jude presents to us that which is positive and says,

But ye, beloved, building yourselves up
on your most holy faith ...

What is the "most holy faith"? At the beginning of this letter, Jude said: "Using all diligence to write to you of our common salvation, I have been obliged to write to you exhorting you to contend earnestly for the faith once delivered to the saints." The "most holy faith" is not a creed. The "most holy faith" is Christ in His totality—"the total Christ," and that is the foundation upon which we are exhorted to build.

In a sense, building up is growing out of the foundation. The Scripture uses two different figures of speech: building a building and growing a tree or a plant. That is why it says in the Scripture, "rooted and grounded in Christ." Christ is the most holy faith, and He is our foundation. Christ is also the root of all things, and therefore we must grow up out of that root and be grounded in Him. So this building up is actually the growing out of the foundation. Also, it is put another way in the Scripture: "Growing up into Christ." We not only grow out of Him, but we are to grow up into Him; that is building. So, on the one hand, building is growing deeper into Christ, and on the other hand, we go higher into Christ. This is "building yourselves up on your most holy faith."

praying in the Holy Spirit

How do we build upon the most holy faith? One of the most effective ways of being built upon the most holy faith is praying in the Holy Spirit. Now praying in the Holy Spirit is very, very much misunderstood. Some people think praying in the Holy Spirit is praying in tongues. There are three different verses which show us the three different aspects of praying. We see the first aspect in I Corinthians 14:14: "For if I pray with a tongue, my spirit prays." When a person's human spirit is touched by the Spirit of God or burdened with a burden from above, and yet there is no understanding because the mind is not involved, the only way for this to be expressed from the spirit is praying in tongues. So praying in tongues is praying with the spirit. My spirit prays, but my understanding is not involved. Because my spirit prays, therefore, I am edified and built up. However, no one else is edified because they do not know what is being prayed.

In Romans 8:26, we see the second aspect. "And in like manner the Spirit joins also its help to our weakness; for we do not know what we should pray for as is fitting, but the spirit itself makes intercession with groanings which cannot be uttered."

Now, this is not praying with my spirit or my spirit praying. It is the Holy Spirit who dwells within me, praying with groanings that cannot be uttered. It is not the person as such or even his spirit. In other words, even my spirit does not know. I do not know what or how to pray. Therefore, the Holy Spirit within me intercedes on my behalf with groanings, using my mouth. Not only is my understanding not involved, but even my spirit does not understand.

When I was in Florida, I was told there was a place where people come together to groan. They would do better to groan in their own homes. It is not the Spirit; it is their own selves, and they do not know what they are groaning for. However, sometimes, there is a place where the Holy Spirit, in a sense, has to take charge because even our spirit is too dull to understand or enter in.

I Corinthians 14 tells us "my spirit prays"; in Romans 8, we learn how the Spirit prays within us; and in Jude, we read about "praying in the Holy Spirit." What is praying in the Holy Spirit? It simply means you are so filled with the Spirit that you are able to cooperate with the Holy Spirit when you pray. In other words, the Holy Spirit is the atmosphere surrounding you, and you are the one who prays there. Your spirit is really cooperating with the Holy Spirit.

Praying in the Holy Spirit is a form (I don't like to use the word form, but I don't have another word) where you find your spirit is able to cooperate fully with the Holy Spirit. The contrast to praying in the Holy Spirit is praying in the flesh. If we live in the flesh, when we pray, we do so in the flesh. You cannot live in the flesh and pray in the Holy Spirit. It is possible that people can live in the flesh and pray with tongues. But praying in the Holy Spirit is very different. You have to live in the Spirit, you have to be filled with the Spirit, and you have to be ruled by the Holy Spirit.

As your life is under the control of the Holy Spirit, your spirit can fully understand what the Spirit is trying to do. Your spirit then is in cooperation with the Holy Spirit to the extent that your understanding is also involved. This kind of praying is the highest form of prayer. When the Holy Spirit prays for you, you are inactive (as in Romans 8). When your spirit is praying, your understanding is passive (as in I Corinthians 14). But here in Jude, by "praying in the Holy Spirit," your whole being is under the control of the Holy Spirit, and you are in full cooperation with the Spirit.

Of course, there is nothing which edifies or builds up more than praying in the Holy Spirit. It will not only build you up but also the whole body. When a person is really cooperating and praying with the Holy Spirit, he is in touch with God. Such prayer builds up the body, brings us closer to the Lord, and gets us deeper in Christ. Thus, praying in the Holy Spirit is one of the most effective means of our being built up in the most holy faith. Then it continues with,

keep yourselves in the love of God

When we are praying in the Holy Spirit, we are actually in union with Christ in the Spirit. Then we keep ourselves in the love of God. Someone has said that God always loves us. The love of God is always there, but to be kept in the love of God is another thing. God always loves us, but are we keeping ourselves in the love of God? In other words, God's love has its terms on this matter of communion. God loves us but are we in the love of God? Are we in constant communion with Him? That means there has to be a life in the Spirit. Therefore, keep yourselves in the love of God. Then we read,

**awaiting the mercy of our Lord Jesus Christ unto
eternal life**

If we keep ourselves in the love of God, no doubt we long for that day when our Lord shall return. So "awaiting the mercy of our Lord Jesus Christ" simply means "expecting His soon return." When He returns, He will bring His mercy to fullness. In the end we discover that it is still mercy; everything is mercy. Therefore, we are looking forward to the mercy of our Lord Jesus unto eternal life, and, of course, that brings us into life in the kingdom. So Jude puts before us a very positive aspect of our Christian life.

We must be built up in the most holy faith. It is not sufficient just to have the foundation laid and not build upon it. That is why we gather together—to be built up together in the most holy faith. We are to be praying in the Holy Spirit, we are to be kept in the love of God together, and we await the mercy of our Lord Jesus Christ unto eternal life. This explains our life together.

May the Lord help us to know that praying is the cooperation of our spirit with the Holy Spirit and the Holy Spirit with our spirit. When our spirit and the Holy Spirit work together, that is praying in the Holy Spirit, and this will keep us in the love of God.

22—Prayer for God's Interest

Colossians 1:9-12—For this reason we also, from the day we heard of your faith and love, do not cease praying and asking for you, to the end that ye may be filled with the full knowledge of his will, in all wisdom and spiritual understanding, so as to walk worthily of the Lord unto all well-pleasing, bearing fruit in every good work, and growing by the true knowledge of God; strengthened with all power according to the might of his glory unto all endurance and longsuffering with joy; giving thanks to the Father, who has made us fit for sharing the portion of the saints in light.

Paul had never been to Colossae or visited the church there, but he heard about them. He said that from the very first day that we heard of the saints in Colossae and of their faith and love, we have not ceased praying and asking for them. I think this is very, very beautiful. Oftentimes, we feel burdened to pray only when we are personally involved. If it is our work or our people, then we feel burdened to pray, but if we are not personally involved and it is only something which we hear secondhand, it is difficult for us to feel burdened to pray. I believe the reason is we are so involved with ourselves that it even shows in our prayer life. If our hearts are really concerned with God's interest, then whether we are personally involved or not really does not matter too much. When we hear something concerning God's work, we will be able to take up the burden and pray. So I believe there is one thing which we need to learn as we are praying together—and that is how to take up burdens and pray for things in which we are not personally involved. We need to ask the Lord to enlarge our hearts that we may be truly concerned with God's interest, and as He does this, then no matter whether we hear or see or are personally involved, all can become to us a burden for prayer.

It is evident that when we are praying together for a brother or sister among us who is sick or has a problem, immediately, many brothers and sisters take up the burden and start to pray. For example, when we are praying for the Lord's will for other places, usually there are only a few prayers. In other words, we are not able to enter into the burden, and it is true if we are not burdened, it is hard to pray. I think we need to ask the question: Why are we not burdened? When Paul heard what happened in Colossae, immediately a burden was created in his heart, and he started to pray.

The second point to note is this: "From the day we heard of your faith and love, do not cease praying and asking for you." Most of the time, when we hear something, we respond with our emotions and pray maybe once, and then we forget. However, Paul said, "We do not cease praying." Now we do not know how long a time had transpired, but evidently, some time had elapsed, and yet Paul was able to continue to pray. Why? Because as long as that burden was not lifted, he did not cease to pray. Actually, this is the way it should be. If we take up a burden, then we should not stop praying until it is lifted—either the answer has come, or the Lord has said "no."

Thirdly, we discover that when Paul took up the burden and continued to pray, he did not just pray in a very general and vague way. His prayer was very definite and with purpose. In other words, praying is not just beating the air; it is hitting a target with definite purpose. Paul knew what he was praying for; he knew what the saints needed, and he prayed accordingly. Therefore he said, "to the end." Paul felt God had something to accomplish in the lives of these saints, and it was to that end that he was praying. His prayer was that they might be filled with the full knowledge of God's will. Now they had faith and love. Evidently, they knew God, but they were not filled with the full knowledge of God's will. Is it not true that this is the condition of God's people everywhere? We know Him, and we may know some of His will, but we are not filled with the full knowledge of His will. In other words, Paul's prayer was for their fullness, their maturity, and their entering fully into the purpose of God in all wisdom and spiritual understanding. Full, fill, all—now these are not ordinary words. Paul was not praying a small prayer as if people get saved, and that is enough; it was for the fullness in all wisdom and understanding. Of course, we know wisdom is that which is in God's mind; understanding is being able to comprehend what God really wants—the ultimate purpose, the will of God. He was praying for their full growth.

In the background of Colossae at that time, we discover there was some kind of agnosticism and mysticism that had invaded the church there. These people came to them trying to persuade them that they were the elite and only they knew the mystery. They began to spread teachings in their midst that were a type of mysticism, asceticism, and agnosticism combined. So Paul, knowing that kind of situation, felt the only way to combat and overcome such things was to be filled

117

with the full knowledge of God. If they were filled with the full knowledge of God's will, then they would not be deceived and distracted by other things. Such knowledge of God is very practical—not like that of the gnostics and the other people. Their knowledge is speculative, impractical, imaginative. It does not affect your life. As a matter of fact, it even loosens your life; and that was what happened. Therefore, Paul prayed "that ye may be filled with the full knowledge of His will, in all wisdom and spiritual understanding, so as to walk worthily of the Lord unto all well-pleasing, bearing fruit in every good work, and growing by the true knowledge of God; strengthened with all power according to the might of his glory unto all endurance and longsuffering with joy; giving thanks to the Father, who has made us fit for sharing the portion of the saints in light." Such knowledge is most practical, enabling us to walk worthily of the Lord, to bear fruit, to grow, to suffer long; it strengthens us; it helps us to give thanks unto the Lord, bringing us into that participation of our inheritance with all the saints in light.

I do feel that as we are learning to pray and work together with God, it is important that we ask the Lord to enlarge our capacity. If the Lord allows us to hear something that is related to His interest (even if we are not personally in touch), it is a call to pray so that we might take these things up and bring them to the Lord, learning how to persevere in prayer. It is not just praying once, and then we forget. Now on Wednesday nights, we may mention a few things for prayer; some may be old subjects and some new. Even if there may be things that are not mentioned, certainly in our private prayers, we must continue to hold these things before the Lord to see that they are being fulfilled according to God's will. As we pray, it should be definite, and it should be for the ultimate purpose. This is working with God, who always works with the ultimate in view, and we should not be satisfied with less than that. We should pray for our brothers and sisters and also ourselves.

23—A Prayerful Attitude

I Thessalonians 5:17—Pray unceasingly.

Probably we have the idea that such an exhortation or command must be given to a church that has matured greatly or to believers who have grown quite a lot; but on the contrary, we find that these two words were given to a young church—the church in Thessalonica. The believers were also young, yet to them was this word "pray unceasingly" given. I wonder if it surprises you that we are exhorted to pray unceasingly. Now, of course, we cannot stay in our closet, close our eyes and be on our knees and pray day and night. That is impossible. Even though there are people who give themselves to intercessory prayer, yet they still have duties to perform, which means they are not able to be on their knees all the time. It is impossible. It cannot be done, yet we are told to pray unceasingly. Therefore, it is clear that what is exhorted here is that prayer is an attitude. That is the only possible way to pray unceasingly. If it is a matter of form, or time, or place, then no one can pray unceasingly. But when we consider this as a matter of spiritual attitude, then it is possible and can be done.

We often say that prayer is like breathing because wherever we are, at any time, whether we are conscious or even unconscious, we breathe. Sometimes we are conscious of our breathing, such as after running a mile. At other times, when we are at home sitting and reading, we are not conscious that we are breathing at all, but we are. Prayer is our spiritual breathing. As breath is essential to our physical life, so prayer is vital to our spiritual life. We must pray and pray unceasingly. We must always have a prayerful attitude. What Paul has emphasized here is this matter of a prayer life—whether we have a prayer life or not.

How is our prayer life? Do we have set times for prayer? Is prayer the first thing in the morning and the last thing at night? The psalmist said he prayed three times a day, and we find Daniel opened the window towards Jerusalem and prayed three times a day. Now it is true a prayer life is more than just having a set time to pray, but to have a set time is basic, essential, and conducive to our prayer life. In other words, we can be so super-spiritual—thinking that we have to pray unceasingly—that we do not need to have any set times because we are praying all the time. If that is what you are thinking, the result is that you are not praying at all. We have to begin with the set time of prayer. In our daily life, we need to set apart a certain time for prayer, whether it is early in the morning or another time. If we cannot do this, then we will not be able to reach the place of praying unceasingly. However, after we have our set time or times of prayer, it does not mean that this is all there is to our prayer life. This set time helps and produces in us that prayerful attitude throughout the day so that wherever and whenever something happens, it becomes natural and spontaneous for us just to lift up our hearts towards the Lord.

Let us consider Nehemiah's prayer life. When he heard that his brethren in Jerusalem were in trouble, he gave himself to prayer. He fasted and prayed, but he had to carry on his duty before the king as cupbearer. One day the king noticed that his face was sad, and this was not something allowed in the court. The king asked: "Why is your face sad? Do you have something on your heart?" Of course, that terrified Nehemiah because in those days, the kings were tyrants, and they were always afraid that someone would do something against them, even murder them. But the Bible says that Nehemiah mentioned to the king what was on his heart, and it was then the king said, "What do you want?" Now the word reads that Nehemiah prayed to the God of the heavens. Of course, he could not close his eyes and say, "Wait a minute and let me pray." As he was standing before the king, he asked Nehemiah that question, and he had to answer right away, but even during that split second, he could still pray to the God of the heavens. He just lifted his heart up; it is an attitude. Nevertheless, to Nehemiah, it was so natural that he did not need to be reminded that he had not yet prayed. It was natural to him because he had developed a life of prayer.

I believe this is important for us in that our corporate prayer cannot rise above the level of our personal prayer life. How can we strengthen our corporate prayer? The important thing is that every one of us must have a prayer life. If our prayer life is weak, when we come together to pray, then our prayers will have to be weak because corporate prayer cannot rise above the level of the sum of our prayer lives. If we want to have strong church prayers, then we have to deepen our prayer life. We need to examine ourselves as to how much time we spend before the Lord in prayer. Do we have a set time or times for prayer? We must ask the Lord to show us if and when things happen, if it is spontaneous and natural for us to lift our hearts toward the Lord, or if our first reaction is to think of how *we* can deal with the situation. These are the things for which we must be before the Lord; otherwise, no matter how we try to strengthen this prayer time, it will be weak. We must cultivate the holy habit of lifting up our hearts to the Lord at any time, at all times, at every occasion, and at every event until it becomes a habit and not something of which we have to be reminded. It will be natural for us to turn our hearts to the Lord, and that is what it means—pray unceasingly.

This is not an exhortation to mature Christians. This is an exhortation, and even a command for young Christians. We have to start when we are young to cultivate the holy habit of prayer. It becomes natural for us to turn everything into prayer. You do not need to close your eyes. You may not be able to when you are driving (and it is better that you don't), but you can still lift your heart to the Lord and pray, and you will find that the Lord answers your prayer.

Sometimes when we come together to pray, it is difficult to take up burdens. In other words, if the Lord has burdened you with something, it is easy for you to take it up personally and pray. However, when you come together with your brothers and sisters and the thing mentioned is not your burden, it becomes very difficult to enter in. Why is it so? In our daily life, if we can turn what we hear, what we see, and whatever we encounter into prayer, then it should not be a difficult thing that when things are mentioned for prayer, we can take them up very quickly and easily as burdens. Therefore, we need to learn to take up burdens in our daily life and not wait until the prayer meeting; it is too late then. As we do this daily, it will cultivate the habit of praying unceasingly; and it is only by doing this that we are able to fulfill our ministry as priests before God because there are so many things for which we must pray. We do not have the time unless we pray unceasingly and maintain a prayerful attitude before the Lord with our hearts open to Him, ready and dependent upon Him. We dare not trust in ourselves, but knowing He is trustworthy, we can turn everything into prayer and just cast our burdens before His feet, and He will not allow us to be moved.

In view of all of this, I feel that it is important for every one of us to re-examine our individual, personal prayer life, looking to the Lord to strengthen it so that we may learn to pray unceasingly and have a prayerful attitude. Then when we come together, it is very easy for us to enter into prayer.

This is not only true when we pray together but also when we pray alone. Sometimes we need to spend time to prepare ourselves to pray because we are not ready. However, if we will always have a prayerful attitude, we will not need to spend time in preparing ourselves to pray; we can enter into prayer right away. May the Lord help us in this respect.

24—Praying Through

Matthew 7:7—Ask, and it shall be given to you. Seek, and ye shall find. Knock, and it shall be opened to you.

Luke 18:1-8—And he spoke also a parable to them to the purport that they should always pray and not faint, saying, There was a judge in a city, not fearing God and not respecting man: and there was a widow in that city, and she came to him, saying, Avenge me of mine adverse party. And he would not for a time; but afterwards he said within himself, If even I fear not God and respect not man, at any rate because this widow annoys me I will avenge her, that she may not by perpetually coming completely harass me. And the Lord said, Hear what the unjust judge says. And shall not God at all avenge his elect, who cry to him day and night, and he bears long as to them? I say unto you that he will avenge them speedily. But when the Son of man comes, shall he indeed find faith on the earth?

We mentioned last time that our praying together can never rise above the level of our personal, private prayers. In other words, if we have a real prayer life in our private life, then when we come together to pray, our corporate prayer will be strong. Otherwise, it will be weak. We need to pray without ceasing, cultivating an attitude of always looking to the Lord and waiting upon Him with a prayerful attitude. This should be our prayer life.

Now I would like to mention something else which is important in both our personal and corporate prayer life which is praying to the end or praying through. We should not just pray and cease. Praying without ceasing not only speaks of always praying but continuing to pray until we receive the answer. Oftentimes, our problem is that we pray for something either privately or publicly, and then we just stop praying altogether. It is no wonder that we find our prayers are not answered as they should.

In Matthew 7:7, there is a simple exhortation on this matter of prayer: "Ask, and it shall be given to you. Seek, and ye shall find. Knock, and it shall be opened to you." In the original, it means to keep on asking, and it shall be given to you, keep on seeking, and ye shall find, keep on knocking and it shall be opened to you. This verse shows us that we need to not just ask once and drop it, not just seek for a moment and then go somewhere else, not just knock once and disappear before the door is opened. If there is something that you feel is a legitimate need and not a luxury, then you should ask your heavenly Father and keep on asking until it is given because immediately following this verse, there is the asking for bread and fish, which are necessities. Sometimes, we ask and keep on asking, and it is not given. When such a situation happens, we probably need to move to the second stage of prayer, which is seeking.

We need to seek the Lord's mind as to why our asking is not answered. Is it because we have asked amiss, or is it because there is something in our lives which the Lord is trying to show us? Sometimes when we ask, and the answer is not forthcoming, then it is time to examine ourselves before the Lord. Maybe the Lord is trying to say something to us. Now, this is seeking—this is not asking—seeking to know the mind of the Lord. After we have determined the Lord's mind, then we can move on to the third stage of prayer, which is knocking.

Now we do not knock on the wall; we knock on the door. In other words, after we know the will of God and we begin to see His way, then it becomes a door. So we know this is the way that God will work, and we knock at the door and keep on knocking until it is opened to us. I think the whole verse teaches us that we need to pray through. As we begin to pray, we are not to stop in the stage of asking, but we may have to go on to seeking and then finally to knocking. When we have begun to knock, we have already found the door; therefore, knowing the will of God, we keep on knocking, and it will be opened to us.

I believe the parable in Luke 18 speaks of the same thing. The Lord said we should always pray and not faint, which means not just praying once and then giving up, thinking that it is hopeless. The Lord used this parable which is an extreme case. It is a contrast—the unjust judge is just the opposite of our heavenly Father. This widow had a need, and she was not ashamed to continue to ask, continue to seek, and continue to knock until that unjust judge could not bear it any longer and avenged her of her adversary. It is used as a contrast because we know that our heavenly Father is so willing to hear us, so ready to give to us, so available, and always wanting to bring us to the ultimate. Surely if we keep on praying, keep on asking, keep on seeking and keep on knocking, He will very quickly open the door for us. Now, this is faith: believing that He will answer; therefore, we keep on and will not give up.

Another example of this is found in the life of Abraham. When God revealed to him His mind concerning Sodom and Gomorrah, Abraham immediately took this matter up in prayer. Abraham said: "Wilt Thou also cause the righteous to perish with the wicked? There are perhaps fifty righteous within the city: wilt Thou also destroy and not forgive the place for the sake of the fifty righteous that are therein? Will not the Judge of all the earth do right?" The Lord answered, "If I find in Sodom fifty righteous within the city, then I will forgive the whole place for their sakes." We know that Abraham continued on with forty-five, forty, thirty, twenty until he came to ten. In other words, he kept on asking, kept on seeking, kept on knocking. Even though there were not even ten righteous in the city and the city was destroyed, Abraham's prayer was answered because God delivered Lot out of Sodom.

Also, we find the same thing in the case of Elijah. After that victory on Mt. Carmel, Elijah went to the top of the mount and prayed for rain. He prayed seven times—not just once. He sent his servant to see if there was any sign of rain, and six times there was nothing; but on the seventh, there was a dark cloud like a hand. The prayer was heard. We must keep on asking! We must pray through! Do not give up!

In the garden of Gethsemane, our Lord Jesus prayed three times until He had prayed through and knew the will of the Father. Paul did the same thing. Three times he prayed over this matter of the thorn in his flesh until he got the answer: "My grace is sufficient for thee."

Throughout the Scripture, we discover that there is one lesson that we need to learn if we want our prayers to be effective—and that is, we must pray things through. Otherwise, we will just touch the surface, skip around and then go on. We may pray for one thing today and another tomorrow, not even waiting for an answer, and this can be true in the prayer meeting. Now probably, when we go over the same thing a few times, people might feel a little tired or faint and wonder why we should do this. But the question is: Have we prayed through? It is much better that we take up fewer matters and see them through than to go around the world and pray for everything and never wait for an answer. I feel this is a danger in a prayer time. Oftentimes, we try to touch so many things all around the world and pray just once, and then it is forever forgotten. In that way, we will never learn to pray through. Whether the answer is yes or no, we must pray through. We have to pray until the Lord says, "That is enough;" for example, when Moses pleaded with the Lord to let him go into Canaan and the Lord had to tell him not to ask anymore. Now, if it comes to that point, then we will stop praying because that is a "no" answer.

When the Lord does give a burden, we should pray through. We may not be able to pray week after week over the same things, but I do feel that we, who are at the prayer meeting, should not be so forgetful concerning the things which have been mentioned for prayer. We should take these into our hearts and, in our private prayers, continue on praying over them until we see the answer.

May the Lord help us to learn to pray and pray through!

25—Ground for Prayer: Friends

Luke 11:5-8—And he said to them, Who among you shall have a friend, and shall go to him at midnight and say to him, Friend, let me have three loaves, since a friend of mine on a journey is come to me, and I have nothing to set before him; and he within answering should say, Do not disturb me; the door is already shut, and my children are with me in bed; I cannot rise up to give it thee? I say to you, Although he will not get up and give them to him because he is friend, because of his shamelessness, at any rate, he will rise and give him as many as he wants.

Our Lord was praying in a certain place, and when He had ceased, His disciples asked Him to teach them to pray. As they watched our Lord Jesus, they sensed that the way He prayed was different from John the Baptist. It was not only different in what He prayed but also in the manner and spirit in which He prayed. The whole atmosphere was different. Therefore, they asked the Lord to teach them to pray, and they asked in such a way that it was as if they had never prayed before.

Then the Lord began to teach them, and in this passage, we see first that He taught them what to pray for. This prayer generally is called the Lord's prayer, but actually, it is the church's prayer. After that, He continued teaching them how to pray, and the "how" is actually found in the parable which we have just read. Then the third section is in verses 9-10 in which He emphasized: "for every one that asks receives; and he that seeks finds; and to him that knocks, it will be opened."

For this time, we will just concentrate on the middle section, which is how to pray. Our Lord used a parable of a friend going to a friend and asking for help for another friend of his. We have three different friends here: the one who prayed, the one to whom he prayed, and the one for whom he prayed. This shows us that there is a relationship in prayer not only of the Father and the children, which we find in the so-called Lord's prayer but there is the more mature one that we find here, which is a relationship of friends. God is willing to take us as His friends. What a condescension that must be! You know, to be friends, there needs to be equality. (There may be a better word, but for the moment, this one comes to mind.) In other words, to be friends, there needs to be a sameness where you can really share with one another; but here, God condescends himself to be our Friend. We are His friends.

You remember our Lord spoke of this in John 15:15. It is true we are His bondslaves. He can command us to do whatever He wants without any explanation. We have to give Him absolute obedience as bondslaves, but the Lord said, "I call you no longer bondmen, for the bondman does not know what his master is doing, but I have called you friends." The Lord is willing to share His secrets with us. Think of that! We have a relationship with the Lord of friendship and fellowship. There is a sharing of thoughts, a sharing of burdens, a sharing of everything. In Proverbs 18:24, it says, "But there is a friend that sticketh closer than a brother." This is our God; He is our Friend. He sticks to us closer than our brother in the flesh.

This parable tells us of a man going at midnight to knock upon the door of his friend. If God makes us His friend, then we should be friends to others. This man did not go to his friend for his own need; he went to him for the need of the other friend. Notice that he went at midnight. Why? Because as a friend, he knew he would not be refused. Now, do we dare to knock at the door of someone at midnight, asking for something? That is the wrong time, but if your friendship is deep, you may knock upon your friend's door at any time and have the assurance that he will open it.

First, we see there is a friendship between God and us. He is willing to be our Friend, and because of that, we dare to come to Him, even at midnight, to knock upon His door, believing it will be opened.

Another point to consider here is this: This friend had a friend coming to him, probably late at night, and he had nothing to put on the table. However, his friendship with that person was so deep that he could not bear to see him hungry, and that is why he went to his friend, asking for three loaves. Is our concern for our friend as deep? Probably we would knock at the door of a friend at midnight for our own need, but will we do this for the need of our friend? Since God shows such friendship to us, should we not show more friendship to our friends? It is true that we do not have anything to put on the table. All we have is a heart, a willingness, a desire for our friend. We have to go to our Father, our God, for the supply. When someone who is our friend in the Lord has a need, we often feel it deeply within because a friendship is there, but we realize we have nothing to put on the table. The supply is not in us; it is in God. We do thank Him that we can go to Him as friends and ask for the supply for our friend. That is one of the reasons the Scripture says, "And pray for one another" (James 5:16). We see that the prayer is answered because of the friendship, but the Lord goes a little bit further.

"And he within answering should say, Do not disturb me; The door is already shut, and my children are with me in bed; I cannot rise up to give it thee? I say to you, Although he will not get up and give them to him because he is his friend, because of his shamelessness, at any rate, he will rise and give him as many as he wants."

Note that it says, "because of his shamelessness." Now isn't it a shame that you should knock upon the door of your friend at midnight? Aren't you ashamed that you continue to knock, refuse to go away when the door is not opened? Therefore, even if the friendship will not do because of his shamelessness, he will have to get up and open the door and give him as much as he wants. The Lord encourages us how to pray. We pray as friends, but we even go further than that. We pray shamelessly!

Sometimes our prayer is too shallow. We dare not harass our Lord. Now dare we to pray? Dare we to open our mouth wide? Do we dare to continue to pray and come to Him and refuse to be refused? Are we so daring? The Lord wants to teach us this: Be shameless when we come to the matter of prayer. Well, in other things, be shameful, but in prayer, be bold. Let us be bold but not presumptuous.

Many years ago, I heard something which I cannot forget. One brother said something had happened between him and another brother, but the other brother said, "It does not matter because our friendship can stand it." That is the attitude we should see in our God. No matter what happens,

His friendship stands. He will defend us. He will give us as much as we need and will not refuse us.

Following this parable are these words: "Ask, and it shall be given to you." In the original, it says: "Ask and keep on asking, seek and keep on seeking, knock and keep on knocking. For, he who keeps on asking shall receive." Often when we come to the door, we dare not knock, and if we do, we knock softly; but let us knock and keep on knocking. Be shameless and it shall be opened. May the Lord help us to be shameless as we come to the best of His grace.

26—Ground for Prayer: Little Children

Luke 11:11-13—But of whom of you that is a father shall a son ask bread, and the father shall give him a stone? or also a fish, and instead of a fish shall give him a serpent? or if also he shall ask an egg, shall give him a scorpion? If therefore ye, being evil, know how to give good gifts to your children, how much rather shall the Father who is of heaven give the Holy Spirit to them that ask him?

Prayer is based on relationship, and without that, there is no ground to pray and no assurance for the answer. In the Old Testament era (and it is true even today), so far as the world was concerned, the only relationship it had with God was the relationship with the Creator and the created. That was the only ground on which man could pray to God. However, the children of Israel in the Old Testament had a better relationship with God because He was not only their Creator but also their covenant God. In the New Testament, with the coming of our Lord Jesus and through His death and resurrection, we are given a new relationship. It is one of Father and son because we remember the words of our Lord Jesus after He was resurrected: "Go to my brethren and say to them, I ascend to my Father and your Father, and to my God and your God" (John 20:17).

Today, this relationship of Father and children is the basic ground on which we pray. In John 1:12, it says, "But as many as received him, to them gave he the right to be children of God." We are given this right, this authority as children of God; we have authority over God. Of course, we have to understand what it means. It is just like when children are born into a family. In a sense, they have some kind of authority over their parents; and the right understanding of that authority is not to rule or lord over, but rather they can claim certain rights with their parents. They can ask for supplies, sustenance, and protection. These rights of the children are, in a sense, authority. Now we know that our God has absolute authority over us because we belong to Him, but since we are His children, we have some claim that we can rightfully claim over Him. We can come to Him with authority, almost like demanding, but I would rather say claiming.

One of our rights is prayer. We have the right to come to our Father to pray; this is our birthright, and there is no need to hesitate or be afraid. We can make a claim upon Him. This is the authority He has given to us, and if we do not pray, it will be like not exercising our rights or our authority. We are encouraged to pray and to ask, and our Lord does this by using this illustration of a son asking for bread from his father. The son has a need; therefore, He asks for bread. Will the father give him a stone instead of the bread? Impossible! If he should ask for fish, will the father give him a serpent? Never! If he should ask for an egg, will the father give him a scorpion? It cannot be! Sometimes the child may ask amiss, ask the wrong thing, and because of that, the father may withhold the wrong thing for which he asked. But even if he should ask wrongly, the father may give him the right thing, and certainly, the reverse is impossible. If the child should ask for the right things—bread, fish and egg, necessities of life—the father will never withhold these from his son. He will never make a substitute that will be hurtful and harmful to his own child. That is impossible.

The Lord used this illustration to show us that, even though we are evil, when we come to the matter of the relationship of father and son, in spite of our being evil, we still know how to give good gifts to our children. We love our children; we give them good gifts and will not purposely hurt or harm them. It is true that sometimes we inadvertently do that, but it is not our desire. So how much more will God, who is good, give the Holy Spirit to those that ask Him. For the Lord said, "No one is good but one, that is God."

In James 4, we are told, "ye have not because ye ask not." Oftentimes, we do not have, and the reason for this is because we do not ask. The Lord used this illustration to show us that if we have legitimate needs, whether they are spiritual or physical, we should ask of our Father. If we do not ask, we do not have; but if we ask, it shall be given to us. Now perhaps we do ask and do not receive, then it is because we sometimes ask amiss. We want to indulge our flesh, and the Lord knows better and does not want us to fall into such indulgence. Therefore, He withholds that thing for which we asked. Surely, if this is our need—whether spiritual or physical— because we are His children and He is our Father, we have the authority to come to Him and claim, and He will not refuse us.

As we see in Luke 11:13, there is something more that the Lord wants to give us. The Bible says, "How much rather shall the Father who is of heaven give the Holy Spirit to them that ask him?" There are two different ways to look at this verse. One way is that it means when asking the Father for the Holy Spirit, how much more He will give the Holy Spirit to you. Another way is when you are asking for bread, He will give you the Holy Spirit and the bread. You are asking for fish; He will give you the Holy Spirit with the fish. You are asking for an egg; He will give you the Holy Spirit and the egg. Now, this is our heavenly Father.

Sometimes, when we are praying for a certain need, probably all we expect is for that need to be met. For example, suppose we are asking for healing; therefore, all we expect is healing. Maybe we are praying for expansion, and that is all we expect, or we are praying for a conference, and all we expect is that there will be one. This is not the way that God works because if we ask for healing, the Father will give us not only healing but the Holy Spirit. What will healing be if He does not give us the Holy Spirit? When we are praying for something, we find that God first gives us the Holy Spirit to convict, to search, and to bring us to a right relationship with Him so that we may be filled with His Spirit. Following that, there will be healing or whatever we ask.

The same thing is true if we ask for expansion. Don't just expect physical expansion. First of all, He will give us the Holy Spirit, and when the Holy Spirit is given, we may have to repent. This might be unexpected because we are praying for expansion. But God, in answering us as Father, will give us the Holy Spirit to bring us to conviction. He will do something more than just give us expansion. Suppose we are expanded physically, and the Holy Spirit is not with us, then what is added would just be an external, temporary, empty thing that would cause more trouble. Therefore, He will give us the Holy Spirit, and we thank God for that.

When God gives us the Holy Spirit, we can expect anything to happen; He will surprise us because He moves on higher ground. This is the way God answers prayer as our Father, and that is the best gift. It is better than bread or fish or egg, for we know that after He gives the Holy Spirit, there will be bread, fish, and egg. Of course, sometimes we come to Him as friends, as we said last week; but at the very basis of all relationships, there is the one of Father and children. So let us come to Him as little children, believing and trusting that if we ask that which is legitimate in His eyes according to His will, He will give it to us. But remember, He will give us the Holy Spirit with what we ask.

27—Ground for Prayer: God's Word

Matthew 15:21-28—And Jesus, going forth from thence, went away into the parts of Tyre and Sidon; and lo, a Canaanitish woman, coming out from those borders, cried to him saying, Have pity on me, Lord, Son of David; my daughter is miserably possessed by a demon. But he did not answer her a word. And his disciples came to him and asked him, saying, Dismiss her, for she cries after us. But he answering said, I have not been sent save to the lost sheep of Israel's house. But she came and did him homage, saying, Lord, help me. But he answering said, It is not well to take the bread of the children and cast it to the dogs. But she said, Yea, Lord; for even the dogs eat of the crumbs which fall from the table of their masters. Then Jesus answering said to her, O woman, thy faith is great. Be it to thee as thou desirest. And her daughter was healed from that hour.

We mentioned before that prayer is based on relationships. If there is the right relationship, then there is the ground to pray. We have a relationship with God our Father, and, as children, we have the right or the authority to ask and to pray to our heavenly Father. We also mentioned that our relationship with the Lord is a kind of friendship. He calls us friends and, as a Friend that sticks closer than a brother, certainly He will rise up and answer all our prayers.

Now I would like to say something different. It is true that prayer is based on relationship, but there is something that is not relationship, and yet it can be ground for our prayer. I do not know the right word, but I will try to use the word concession. What is concession? One dictionary gives the definition as "grace." So what is grace? It is said that grace is "a concession that cannot be claimed as a right." In other words, if it is a right, we have the right to ask for it, and that is not a concession. A concession cannot be claimed as a right, but it is something given to us as a favor. I believe that the Lord does show us in His word how He makes many concessions for us in order to encourage us to pray. Even if the relationship is not there, over, above, and beyond relationship, God condescends to give us a number of concessions. Of course, we know the relationship is always there. All of these concessions are like handles which we can hold and turn. One of these concessions on prayer is given in this particular Scripture which we have read.

A Canaanitish woman came to Jesus and said, "Have pity on me, Lord, Son of David." Now, as a Canaanitish woman, she had no right to the Lord, especially when she addressed Him as Son of David. What has the Son of David to do with a Canaanitish woman because He was sent to the lost sheep of the house of Israel. So this woman had absolutely no claim upon the Lord. No wonder she cried and cried, but the Lord did not say a word. The woman cried so much that the disciples became disturbed. They thought this was very much unlike the Lord because whenever people cried, the Lord always responded right away, and sometimes before they cried, He would respond. However, in this particular case, the Lord acted very strangely. Therefore, the disciples asked the

Lord to do something. They said that if He was not going to respond to her cry, then dismiss her, let her go, and tell her there is nothing for her. It was at this moment that our Lord explained.

He told them that the Son of David was sent to the lost sheep of the house of Israel—not for the Gentiles. In other words, this woman had no claim upon Him as the Son of David. Then the woman said, "Lord, help me." Notice there is a little change here; instead of saying "Son of David," she said, "Lord." So the Lord began to answer in the same way He answered the disciples: "It is not well to take the bread of the children and cast it to the dogs." We know that the Jews looked upon the Gentiles as unclean and therefore called them dogs. The Jews were clean because they only ate clean food, according to Leviticus. The Lord said that He was sent to the house of Israel, and He was to give bread to the children of Israel—not to the dogs. There was no relationship. But when the Lord said "dogs," He used a different word. It was not the wild dogs but the little dogs, pet dogs, domesticated ones. So the Lord gave a concession to this woman. As far as relationship was concerned, there was none. The Lord said, "It is true you are not of the house of Israel, but I consider you as a pet dog, a dog that belongs to the house." Immediately, the woman took hold of that word and acknowledged, "I am a dog." (I think this is important because we need to realize what we are. Oftentimes, when we come to the Lord, we do not know what we are. We think we deserve something and have a right. However, when we realize that actually, we have no right, we realize that we do not deserve to eat at the table, but certainly, we can pick up some crumbs under the table. The Lord has given us a concession because we are created by

Him and therefore belong to Him, not as children, but as dogs.) The woman just took hold of the word of God as a handle and turned it as a key which unlocks a door, and it opened. The Lord said, "O woman, thy faith is great." In other words, she knew how to humble herself before the Lord and lay hold of the concession which God had given her, and the concession here was the word of our Lord Jesus. If our Lord had kept silent, that woman would have been finished; but He opened His mouth, and even though outwardly it sounded harsh, it was actually the Lord opening a way for her. Through that word as a concession the woman took hold of it and her request was granted. You will find this in many places in the Bible.

When we come to pray, thank God we have more than one relationship; however, very often, it will help us greatly if we know how to lay hold of the word of God during these prayer times. The word of God is His concession to us. If He keeps silent, we do not know what He will do or not do; we do not know His will. But if He speaks—and He has spoken—then His word is a concession to us. It is grace. As we learn to lay hold of God's word, we will find our prayer time will be more effective.

For instance, in the book of Exodus, it is recorded that Moses went up to the mountain to intercede for the children of Israel after they had sinned against God. God had already said He would destroy the whole nation and raise up Moses' seed to be a nation, but Moses pleaded with God on two grounds: (1) The Name of the Lord. "What will happen to Your Name? You delivered the children of Israel out of Egypt with a strong arm, and now You want to destroy them. What will the Egyptians say? It will reflect upon Your Name." This is another concession that we can lay hold of in our pleadings with God—His Name. (2) The word of God. Moses pleaded with God saying: "You promised Abraham, Isaac, and Jacob and swore to them that You would multiply their seed and give the land to them as their inheritance. Here is Your word; You cannot deny Yourself; You cannot go back on Your word; You have to do what You say." So Moses used God's own word, and the Bible records that God repented of the evil that He had decided to do to the children of Israel.

We find the same thing in the prayers of Nehemiah and others in the Scripture—people who truly knew how to pray, how to intercede, how to lay hold of God's concession and His word.

It is always good if we can remind God of what He has said when we pray. If we know how to do this, it will give effect to our prayers. So I hope the Holy Spirit will quicken God's word to our heart, and as His word is given to us, We can use it as a handle in our prayers.

God's concession is His grace!

28—Have the Faith of God

Mark 11:22-24—And Jesus answering says to them, Have faith in God. Verily I say to you, that whosoever shall say to this mountain, Be thou taken away and cast into the sea, and shall not doubt in his heart, but believe that what he says takes place, whatever he shall say shall come to pass for him. For this reason I say to you, All things whatsoever ye pray for and ask, believe that ye receive it, and it shall come to pass for you.

Jesus is teaching here a very great lesson on prayer. One morning, the Lord Jesus was on His way from Bethany to Jerusalem, and He was hungry. He saw a fig tree full of leaves, but He could not find any fruit on it, so He cursed that fig tree. Now that is the only thing our Lord Jesus cursed during His lifetime. The next morning when they passed by that fig tree, Peter noticed that it had withered, so he said to Him: "Rabbi, see the fig tree which thou cursedst is dried up" (v. 21). The Lord answered, "Have faith in God." Literally, "have faith in God" is "have the faith of God." What is the faith of God? God has faith and what is His faith? He believes that whatever He says is done—that is His faith.

In Genesis, God said, "let there be light," and there was light. God never doubts His own word. When He speaks, it is done. His word is as good as His act. That is the faith of God, and here our Lord Jesus demonstrated that faith. He spoke to the fig tree. He had no doubt that it would be withered, and so it was. Surely it must have been a surprise to

Peter, but to our Lord, it was as natural as it could be because He had spoken.

Our Lord Jesus exhorts us to have that kind of faith—the faith of God. It is not something beyond us, nor is it something which we cannot receive because He said: "have the faith of God." To have the faith of God is not only a possibility, it is a command. In a sense, this is the only genuine and real kind of faith: God's faith. We do not have any faith; it has to be God's faith in us. If we do not have faith, all we see is the mountains that loom high above us, blocking our way and trying to crush us. But if we have God's faith—that is, if we see God and believe in His power, then we can speak to the mountain and command it to be removed to the sea. In other words, the path is clear.

The Lord said, "For this reason I say to you, All things whatsoever ye pray for and ask, believe that ye receive it." In the original, it says, "Believe that ye received it." Not only believe that ye shall receive it but believe that you have received it. You first receive what you pray for in faith, and then you will receive it in fact. You do not wait to receive it until you receive it in fact; but you receive it first in faith and then, according to your faith, shall it be done to you. Now, this is the faith of God. It is not being presumptuous, nor is it a psychological suggestion. It is faith! Of course, we know that whatsoever we ask or pray for is according to His will because when we do this, the Scripture says we have the confidence that He answers us. If we are really one with God and united with Christ and know His will, then when we pray and ask, we ought to believe that we have received it. Otherwise, it is a lack of faith.

There is a difference between faith and hope. Hope is expecting something to happen, but faith is believing it has already happened. Why is this? Because faith is the substantiating of the things hoped for. It is true that this is the thing hoped for, but faith has already substantiated it. Faith is to see what God sees ("whatsoever ye pray for and ask"). In other words, we are uttering for God His word or His will; and if we are uttering for Him, then we ought to believe that we receive it and it shall come to pass. Sometimes we may think it is too difficult for us to exercise such faith. But when you really think about it, you realize anything less than that is not faith; it is hope, but not faith. Faith is believing in God, believing in God's word, believing in God's will, believing in His power, believing that it is done. Now that is faith!

29—Ask in His Name

John 16:23-24, 26-27—And in that day ye shall demand nothing of me: verily, verily, I say to you, Whatsoever ye shall ask the Father in my name, he will give you. Hitherto ye have asked nothing in my name: ask, and ye shall receive, that your joy may be full. In that day ye shall ask in my name; and I say not to you that I will demand of the Father for you, for the Father himself has affection for you, because ye have had affection for me, and have believed that I came out from God.

When our Lord Jesus was with His disciples, they did indeed pray to God; but they looked to the Lord Jesus for all their needs. When He left them, where would they turn? To whom would they turn for their needs? It was here that our Lord said: "In that day, a great change will come (and we know that day is the day of His resurrection). Before that day, you never asked the Father anything in my name; but in that day and onward, that is what you will do. You will ask of My Father in My name, and whatsoever ye shall ask, ye shall receive that your joy may be full." We know that on the day of His resurrection, a new relationship was established. He said, "Go to my brethren and say to them, I ascend to my Father and your Father, and to my God and your God." In other words, through the death and resurrection of Jesus, God is not only our God, He has become our Father. He is the

God and Father of our Lord Jesus, and He is the God and Father of us.

There is a new relationship of Father and children. However, it is not only a new relationship, but the Lord said, "Now you can pray to your Father; you can ask your Father." Why did this happen? Because the Lord said, "You have loved Me and believed in Me; therefore, My Father loves you, and He will hear you." Our love towards the Lord touches the heart of God the Father towards us. There is a new relationship and a new love, and on the basis of this, the Father loves you because you have loved the Lord Jesus. Now we dare to pray; we dare to ask; we dare to approach the throne of grace.

The Lord is encouraging us to pray, but how are we going to pray? How are we going to use our new relationship and new love in our prayers? He said, "in My name." Thus, the key is in My name. If we go to the Father in the name of Jesus, then whatsoever we ask, we will receive. His name is not a formality. Sometimes the customary way of concluding a prayer is: "in His name" or "in the name of the Lord Jesus." But we know that is not a formality; it is a reality. The Lord is now with the Father, but He leaves His name with us, and this is one of His concessions. He leaves His name with us, and His name is as good as His Person or His Presence. We have His name with us, and in His name, we can go to the Father and ask, and the Father will never refuse us, as the Father has never refused His Son.

In the Gospel of John, Jesus said, "Father, I thank thee that thou hast heard me; but I knew that thou always hearest me" (John 11:41b,42a). The Father always heard Him, so when we come in His name, it is almost as if He is praying;

therefore, the Father will never refuse us. His name is so powerful and so precious to the Father that the Father will do any and everything—as He always does—for His Son. This name is a mighty name, and this name is ours! He has given His name to us, and He encourages us to pray in His name. Now, of course, in His name means that we must be one with Him. If we ask something that is contrary to His character or His will, we are not asking in His name. We may use that formula—"in His name, Amen"—but in reality, we are not. We are praying our own prayer; we are asking for our own will; we want what we want instead of being one with Him. The Lord said, "I say not to you that I will demand of the Father for you." Now we know, today, the Lord Jesus is our great High Priest and our great Intercessor; He intercedes for us. But here He said, "I do not tell you that I will pray for you; you pray yourselves." When we pray in His name, it is almost as if He is praying. So far as the Father is concerned, He hears the Son, and, therefore, we shall receive what we ask because of that name.

Of course, "in His name" means further that we must be in subjection to Him and to His authority. It will not be true if we use His name, and yet we do not submit ourselves to His authority. When we submit ourselves completely to His name—that is, to His authority—we will find that our prayer will have power and authority, even with the Father.

Also, in His name means we are praying according to His will, in accordance with His character, and if we do this, we have the confidence that the Father will answer our prayer.

We not only have such a new relationship with God and a new love, but we also have the name of Jesus with us. As we come to pray, we do not come in our own name, for our own will. We come because we have the name of the Lord Jesus, and we are one with Him. We know both His character and His will, and we want His will to be done on earth as it is in heaven. It is therefore encouraging that the Lord said, "Hitherto ye have asked nothing in my name: ask, and ye shall receive, that your joy may be full."

30 — Prayer and God's Character

Genesis 18:16-33 — And the men rose up thence, and looked toward Sodom; and Abraham went with them to conduct them. And Jehovah said, Shall I hide from Abraham what I am doing? Since Abraham shall indeed become a great and mighty nation; and all the nations of the earth shall be blessed in him. For I know him that he will command his children and his household after him, and they shall keep the way of Jehovah, to do righteousness and justice, in order that Jehovah may bring upon Abraham what he hath spoken of him. And Jehovah said, Because the cry of Sodom and Gomorrah is great and their sin is very grievous, I will go down now, and see whether they have done altogether according to the cry of it, which is come to me; and if not, I will know it. And the men turned thence, and went towards Sodom; and Abraham remained yet standing before Jehovah. And Abraham drew near, and said, Wilt thou also cause the righteous to perish with the wicked? There are perhaps fifty righteous within the city: wilt thou also destroy and not forgive the place for the sake of the fifty righteous that are therein? Far be it from thee to do so, to slay the righteous with the wicked, that the righteous should be as the wicked — far be it from thee! Will not the Judge of all the earth do right? And Jehovah said, If I find at Sodom fifty righteous within the city, then I will forgive all the place for their sakes. And Abraham answered and said, Behold now, I have ventured to speak unto the Lord; I, who am dust and ashes. Perhaps there may want five of the fifty righteous: wilt thou destroy all the city on account of the five? And he said, If I shall find forty-five there, I will not destroy it. And he continued yet to speak with him, and said, Perhaps there may be forty found there. And he said, I will not do it for the forty's sake. And he said, Oh, let not the Lord be angry that I speak! Perhaps there may be thirty found there. And he said, I will not do it if I find thirty there. And he said, Behold now, I have ventured to speak with the Lord. Perhaps there may be twenty found there. And he said, I will not destroy it for the twenty's sake. And he said, Oh, let not the Lord be angry, that I speak yet but this time! Perhaps there may be ten found there. And he said, I will not destroy it for the ten's sake. And Jehovah went away when he had ended speaking to Abraham; and Abraham returned to his place.

We find in this chapter that the Lord visited Abraham and brought him some news—one good, the other bad. The good news was that his wife Sarah would have a child, and we can understand why God brought this good news to Abraham because all the promises of God were centered upon that child. Then the Lord shared with Abraham the bad news, which was that the sins of Sodom and Gomorrah had ascended up to heaven, and judgment would come upon these cities.

Now I wonder why the Lord let Abraham hear this bad news. Was it a test of his character? We remember how Lot chose what he considered the better part of the land. He went away from Abraham and moved into the city of Sodom. Abraham even delivered him from the four kings, but Lot still remained there. Could it be that God wanted to test Abraham's character to see how far he would go in his relationship with Lot, how big his heart was? Abraham forgave his nephew and rescued him, but Lot still continued on in his old ways. Would Abraham say, "Well, if that is what you want, you will have it," or was his heart so big that he still had Lot very deeply in his heart?

Now it could have been that God let him hear this bad news for these reasons, but I believe it was something more. God was going to destroy Sodom, but He knew there was one righteous man there, and it was against God's character to destroy the righteous with the wicked. Thus, God shared this news with Abraham because He was mindful of the fact that Abraham knew His character and would plead with Him to deliver Lot out of destruction. In other words, God was looking for someone who understood His character and who would intercede on that basis so that He might do something which would reflect upon Him. I think, probably, this is more the reason than the first one.

Abraham based his intercession all on one point, which was: "Will not the Judge of all the earth do right?" There was no promise, so he could not plead according to God's promise. There was no word, but there was God's character. So in this matter of intercession, sometimes, even if we do not have God's word or His promise, if we know who He is and His character, we can always intercede according to that, and we will be heard because God cannot deny himself. I believe when people begin to plead with God on the ground of His character, probably, that is the deepest ground for intercession. Abraham came to God and said: "Now, Lord, if there are fifty righteous in the city, will you destroy it? Will You destroy the righteous with the wicked? You are the Judge of all. Certainly, You will not do such a thing." Of course, Abraham thought of Lot, no doubt about that. Actually, he was pleading for Lot, but more so for God's own character. He did not want God to do something which would reflect upon His character. He was concerned with God's glory and not just Lot's life, so he continued to plead and plead, and all his pleadings were based on God's character. Even though there were not ten righteous in the city (unfortunately, there was only one), God answered Abraham's prayer and delivered Lot. As a matter of fact, God delivered four. When Lot's wife looked back, she became a pillar of salt, and his two daughters were delivered. But basically, it was Lot whom God delivered because God remembered Abraham and his intercession.

Therefore, when we come together to pray and intercede, there is one thing on which we can always fall back, and that is God's character. Actually, we do not know a person's character until we live close to him, and Abraham lived very close to the Lord. We see that he not only entertained God and the angels, but he went a distance with them, remaining in the presence of the Lord. All of this shows that Abraham was a person who really lived in the presence of the Lord, and because of that, he came to know God's character.

I think there is nothing better in knowing God than knowing His character. You do not know a person until you know his character. To know God is to know His character, and this gives us a responsibility. Such knowledge is not vain; it is very practical. With knowledge such as this, we are called to intercede so that God may not deny himself. I do believe that this is something that we would like to learn as we come together to pray.

31—Prayer and Our Character

James 5:16b—The fervent supplication of the righteous man has much power.

We talked about how the character of God is one of the fundamental grounds for our intercession. We mentioned last time that Abraham pleaded with God for the city of Sodom, and it was on the ground of God's character—a just God. God is just; we can plead on that ground. God is love; we can plead on that ground. God is holy; we can plead on that ground, and we could continue on.

I would like to mention another thing, and that is, our character and prayer. There are two parties involved in prayer—God and ourselves. The character of God is the ground of all intercession, but our character does have something to do with the power of prayer. Now that does not mean we have any merit or that we can approach God on the ground of our merits. We do not have any merit; we are not worthy.

Once, the elders of the Jews came to the Lord concerning the centurion and his servant who was ill, saying, "He is worthy to whom thou shouldest grant this, for he loves our nation, and himself has built the synagogue for us." That was the idea of the elders of the Jews. They thought prayer was based upon a person's merit, but the centurion thought differently. He sent word to Jesus saying: "Lord, do not trouble thyself, for I am not worthy that thou shouldest enter under my roof. Wherefore neither did I count myself worthy to come to thee" (Luke 7:6b, 7a). He really did not think he was worthy at all. He thought: "It is Your mercy; it is Your grace. It is not my merit or my worthiness."

So we can see it is very true that whether we are worthy or not does not enter into the picture when we come to this matter of prayer because we are never worthy. We are made worthy only by the Lord himself and His blood. Therefore, we have to let this go and not have the idea that we deserve to have our prayer heard because we have done some good. Probably, that is our natural thinking—we have behaved very well, so God will hear us. That is our natural thought, and we should not have it in our minds. We are never worthy; it is the worthiness of our Lord Jesus on which we can approach God. This must be clear. Even though we find that our prayer is not based on our worthiness in the Scripture, our character does have something to do with it.

For instance, we have the incident of the blind man who was healed by the Lord, as recorded in John 9. When the Sanhedrin questioned him and asked how his eyes were opened, he mentioned that a Man by the name of Jesus did it. They asked him to give glory to God, saying that they knew Jesus was sinful. The blind man said, "But we know that God does not hear sinners; but if anyone be God-fearing and do his will, him he hears" (John 9:31). Now, this is a truth. Of course, when a sinner offers a penitent prayer, God hears him. Even in extraordinary circumstances, God hears a sinner; but so far as the rule is concerned, God does not hear a sinner but hears the one who fears Him and does His will. That is how character is connected with prayer.

In the book of James, he says that the fervent prayer of the righteous has much power. And the psalmist said in his approach to God, "Hear me because of my righteousness; do not hear the wicked." So, on the one hand, it is not based on our worthiness; yet, on the other hand, our character does have something to do with prayer. Of course, no one is righteous. The righteous are only those who have believed in the Lord Jesus and have been clothed with Christ as their righteousness. In other words, God does not hear a sinner but hears the righteous. We have that position before God, but it is more than that. Thank God for that position of being righteous, but it may be that our condition is not the same as our position. For this reason, when we come to pray, how we need to confess, asking God for forgiveness, how we need the cleansing of the precious blood. We can never approach God in prayer without sensing deeply within us the need for the cleansing of the precious blood because we know that even though we are positionally righteous, we have to be conditionally righteous also. God is righteous, and if there is incompatibility, then we know there is something standing between God and us.

The psalmist said, "Had I regarded iniquity in my heart, the Lord would not hear" (Psalm 66:18). Suppose you are thinking of some iniquity in your heart, and you try to pray, will God hear you? He will not because there is incompatibility. Therefore, even though we are never worthy and merit does not enter into the area of prayer, God does require compatibility with Him. There is a right relationship, an agreement in character that God demands of us. It is true that those who have developed a character of righteousness in their lives do have more power with God in prayer. We do wonder why some people's prayers seem to have much power and others not so much. We know God is fair; He is not partial. So why is this so? I think the reason is that some people have developed a character throughout the years that is compatible with God and, because of that, He loves to hear and answer the prayers of such people. With others, they do pray, and God hears them, but they do not seem to have much power in their prayers. The reason is that something is lacking in their character. It is very important that we not only know the character of God, but also we must develop a Christian character before Him. This is not the basis of prayer, but it has something to do with the power of prayer.

Think of the words of the Lord Jesus: "Father, I thank thee that thou hast heard me; but I knew that thou always hearest me" (John 11:41a,42b). With the Lord Jesus, there was assurance that God always heard Him because He was a Man whose character was compatible. It was the same as the character of God; therefore, there was power in His prayer.

James relates this: "The fervent supplication of the righteous man has much power" (James 5:16b). The emphasis here is not really on the word fervent but on the word righteous. If you read the sentence before it—"Confess therefore your offenses to one another, and pray for one another, that ye may be healed"—I believe it has something to do with the righteous. Therefore, do not think that our lives have nothing to do with our prayer. They have much to do with it because character affects our prayer. Again, let me underline this because we can easily misunderstand, thinking that it gives us ground. No! It does not, but it does give us boldness and power in prayer. May the Lord help us to see that we are not just coming to a prayer meeting, but our lives have much to do with our prayers. If we want our prayers to have power before God, then we need to develop our character. Then we will have boldness and power with God.

32—Prayer and the Meditation of Our Hearts

PSALM 19
To the chief Musician. A Psalm of David.

The heavens declare the glory of God; and the expanse sheweth the work of his hands.

Day unto day uttereth speech, and night unto night sheweth knowledge.

There is no speech and there are no words, yet their voice is heard.

Their line is gone out through all the earth, and their language to the extremity of the world. In them hath he set a tent for the sun,

And he is as a bridegroom going forth from his chamber; he rejoiceth as a strong man to run the race.

His going forth is from the end of the heavens, and his circuit unto the ends of it; and there is nothing hid from the heat thereof.

The law of Jehovah is perfect, restoring the soul; the testimony of Jehovah is sure, making wise the simple;

The precepts of Jehovah are right, rejoicing the heart; the commandment of Jehovah is pure, enlightening the eyes;

The fear of Jehovah is clean, enduring forever; the judgments of Jehovah are truth, they are righteous altogether:

They are more precious than gold, yea, than much fine gold; and sweeter than honey and the dropping of the honeycomb.

Moreover, by them is thy servant enlightened; in keeping them there is great reward.

Who understandeth his errors? Purify me from secret faults.

Keep back thy servant also from presumptuous sins; let them not have dominion over me: then shall I be perfect, and I shall be innocent from great transgression.

Let the words of my mouth and the meditation of my heart be acceptable in thy sight, O Jehovah, my rock, and my redeemer.

When we come together for prayer, it is not just to say a few prayers or go through a religious exercise. It is to expect our prayers to be accepted in the sight of God. Prayers are to be offered with the idea that they are accepted by God. How can our prayers be acceptable in God's sight? I believe it involves two things—the words of our mouth and the meditation of our heart. If we pray with the words of our mouth and they are not rooted in the meditation of our heart, then the words are very superficial. For our prayers to be acceptable in God's sight, we need to be careful about the words of our mouth and also the meditation of our heart.

Of course, we know that we should not be overly careful about the words of our mouth because if we are, then we are composing our own prayer, and prayer is not a composition. Sometimes, we dare not pray because we are afraid that the words of our mouth are not good enough or good composition, but actually, that kind of fear comes from having people in view and not God. In other words, God is not expecting us to have good prayers. If you want to have good prayers which are composed, then read the Prayer Book, and you will find they are very well composed and much better than what we can do, but God is not looking for composition. When we are thinking of composition, it is actually the fear of man; we want people to think our prayers are beautiful, and that is really out of order. We should not be overly careful about the words of our mouth; nevertheless, we do stress that our words are important, as we can see from the Scripture. Sometimes, a word misused makes the prayer unacceptable, such as in the case of the Syrophoenician woman. She addressed the Lord as Son of David, and she was not heard until she said, "Lord."

Why are our words important? It is because they represent our understanding. Out of the fulness of the heart comes our words. We cannot just be careless in what we say to the Lord. We not only have to speak in a humble way, but we have to be careful not to speak the wrong things. That is important, but I think even more important than the words of our mouth is the meditation of our heart. God looks upon our heart; and if our heart is not in it, no matter how many words we utter or how beautiful they are, they will not be acceptable. Our heart must be in our prayer, and that is why it mentions the meditation of our heart. In other words, it is our heart that must meditate.

Modern life is such that meditation is a lost art. People do not meditate. They are always rushing here and there. They do not stop; they do not think; they do not ponder; they do not meditate. For our prayers to be acceptable before the Lord, meditation is essential. It is not only important in reading the Scripture but also in prayer because things on which you have not meditated prove your heart is not there. If your heart is truly there, you will think and think and think over it.

Mary is an example of this in the Scripture. When she heard something which she did not understand, she did not just let the words pass; she kept them in her heart and pondered over them (see Luke 1:29, 2:19). That is meditation.

Sometimes we may offer a prayer, and our meditation measures the depth of our hearts in it. We may mention a subject for prayer, and you pray for it, but you have never pondered before the Lord about the situation. That kind of prayer is very shallow. Things about which you have pondered before the Lord have depth in them when you pray. Your heart is really in it, and it makes your prayer weighty and not just floating around. To have our prayers acceptable, they have to be real, and what makes them real is the combination of these two things: the words of our mouth and the meditation of our heart.

Let us look at it the other way. Sometimes we will meditate a lot, but we never put it in words, and the result is we are always vague, and our thoughts are confused. Words crystallize our thoughts. If we meditate a lot, try to utter it in words so that it becomes very solid and substantial. That makes our prayer real. I believe it is the combination of the words of our mouth and the meditation of our heart that makes real prayer. If you lack in either, you will find something is missing. As we pray, we will discover that the things which we have pondered about before the Lord will have our heart involved in it. Oftentimes, the difficulty is that we do not have the right words to utter the meditation of our heart. In that case, we need to look to the Lord to give us the right words for it. The right word is not only important when we are preaching, it is also important when we are praying. It does have its effect.

Let us look to the Lord that He will so stir our hearts that they will not be careless and insensitive and that we will be able to take up burdens and ponder over the things the Lord has brought to our attention. As we do this, let us ask the Holy Spirit to give us the right words to express it in prayer.

Sometimes, when we are praying, we sense that it does not hit the target. A few prayers may have been offered over the same thing, but they seem to miss. Then someone prays, and suddenly, a word is uttered, and it hits the target, and we know God has heard. Let us learn this before the Lord. Of course, it needs practice; but we thank God the Holy Spirit is with us, and He will teach us how to make our prayers really acceptable with the words of our mouth and the meditation of our heart.

33—Thy Kingdom Come

Matthew 6:10a—Let thy kingdom come.

This so-called Lord's prayer, as we know, is really the church's prayer. Our Lord Jesus teaches His church how to pray. Now surely, it is not His will that we should just repeat these words without really having our heart in them. Here the Lord is showing us what subjects He expects the church to pray, and this one is: "Thy kingdom come." Sometimes, we feel that we are weak in prayer. We have two problems: We do not know what to pray (the subject of prayer), and we do not know how to pray (the way to pray). It is true that the Holy Spirit, as we find in Romans 8, comes to our aid when we do not know what and how to pray (see v. 26). He will intercede within us and for us according to God. The Holy Spirit will not only come to our aid in this matter of prayer, but the very word of God shows us what we need to pray. The Bible gives us all the principles, and the Holy Spirit applies them to specific situations. So one of the things the church should pray is: "Thy kingdom come."

We know that one day the kingdom of this world will become the kingdom of our Lord and of His Christ (see Revelation 11:15). There are different versions and one of them, which is probably closer to the original, says: "The kingdom of the world shall become the kingdom of our Lord and of His Christ." One day the kingdom of God will come upon this earth. The Lord will take over the world and make it His own kingdom. What a tremendous thing that will be. Just think of what the kingdoms of this world are today.

Think of all the nations, all the countries, even the so-called Christian countries, not to mention the heathen countries that one day shall become the kingdom of our Lord and of His Christ. His kingdom shall come upon this earth. What a glorious day that will be, and because of this, the Lord teaches His church to pray for the coming of that kingdom.

Are we praying "Thy kingdom come"? If the Lord did not want us to pray for the coming of His kingdom, then He would not teach us this way, and He would not command us to pray in this fashion. This shows that the heart of our Lord Jesus is in it. How He desires that His kingdom will be manifested upon this earth and righteousness will rule. The kingdom of the world shall become the kingdom of our Lord and of His Christ. He longs for it; therefore, He asks His church to pray for it.

We must not only pray for the kingdom, but we must also seek the kingdom:

But seek ye first the kingdom of God and his righteousness, and all these things shall be added unto you (Matthew 6:33).

This refers to our daily life. In our daily living, we should not always be concerned with what we should eat or drink or with what we should be clothed. Our heavenly Father knows that we have need of these things. We should seek the kingdom of God first, seek His righteousness. This seeking is not just a casual going along. It is really making an effort and putting yourself into it. We really need to seek the kingdom and His righteousness. If we do not seek, we will not have it. The kingdom is for the violent, "and the violent seize on it" (Matthew 11:12b).

In our daily life, we need to seek that His kingdom and His righteousness will be real to us and that we will practice His righteousness. When we are seeking the kingdom, we cannot help but pray for it, and if we pray for it, we will seek it. You cannot separate these two things. If we are not praying for the kingdom, we are probably not seeking it because in seeking the kingdom, we will see that the kingdom of this world is so contrary to the kingdom of God. How difficult it is for us today to really live in the kingdom and practice His righteousness. On the one hand, we must seek the kingdom of God; on the other hand, we must pray, "Thy kingdom come." These two things must go together.

It is true that this is the prayer of the church. The church ought to offer such prayer, whether praying for individuals— their salvation, physical needs, sicknesses, or their problems— or whether praying for a number of other things. If we do not have the kingdom in view, our prayers probably will not hit the mark. Why do we pray for the salvation of souls? It is that the kingdom may come. Why do we pray that the various needs may be supplied? It is that the kingdom may come into their lives. It is not just that people may have their needs met. Whether we are praying for individuals, for the church, for nations, or for the whole world, there must be behind it that one prayer: "Thy kingdom come." This should be the prayer of the church.

Of course, we know that according to the word of God, the kingdom will come even though it does not look like it from the outward appearance. One day the kingdom will be manifested upon this earth, and Christ will reign in righteousness. We know it is coming, but it just does not come suddenly. It does not come out of the blue. Yes, when it does come, it may come very quickly; but before the public manifestation of the kingdom of God, it has to first come spiritually. Then it will come physically upon this earth. We are not only saved, but God has planted us here and there over the whole earth establishing, as it were, the beachheads or the strategic points. Through these people, His kingdom becomes a reality in their midst, and their testimony will affect the unseen world as well as the physical world. Today, this kingdom is hidden among God's people; it is underground. However, this underground kingdom is to undermine the kingdom of this world and bring it to the King of kings and the Lord of lords. This is the way that God will do it; therefore, how we need to pray for this kingdom. We need to seek it and pray for it. If the church is faithful in praying and seeking for the coming of His kingdom, thereby causing His kingdom to become a spiritual reality in the church, then I believe we hasten the coming of the kingdom. What would be the sense of our Lord asking us to pray "Thy kingdom come" if our prayer would not affect the timing of the coming of the kingdom? Because we pray, it must be that the coming of the kingdom is hastened. If we do not pray that prayer, probably the kingdom will be delayed; therefore, the church has a very great responsibility. We must remember: We are not merely praying for some souls to be saved, for some sicknesses to be healed, or some problems to be solved. We are not just praying that the Lord will bless us and use us or praying for this country or that country.

We must have the kingdom in view—*His* kingdom! The subject of our prayer is universal; it is great. Sometimes, our prayers get smaller and smaller, and we begin to forget, but then the Lord puts a burden upon the church to pray for something big, even the kingdom of God. Of course, within this are included all the tiny details, but do not lose sight of the kingdom.

Our hearts do long and cry out: "Thy kingdom come." We are entering into the very end of this age, and in view of all the difficult situations, we realize that the world is not getting better; it is getting worse. The conflict is not getting smaller; it is getting bigger. It is more difficult for us today to live as a Christian than it was fifty years ago, and because of this, it should move us to really pray, "Thy kingdom come." This is our only hope! God has not called us to reform the world, but He has called us to be a testimony for Him that one day this world will surrender to the sovereignty and kingship of Christ. No matter what the various things for which we are praying might be, may we not lose sight of that subject the Lord wants His church to pray: "Thy kingdom come!"

34—Thy Will Be Done

Matthew 6:10—Let thy will be done as in heaven so upon the earth.

As we continue to consider this so-called Lord's prayer, we see that it is the Lord teaching His church to pray, and we should really take up the burden and the spirit of this prayer. Last time we mentioned that the church should pray, "Thy kingdom come," and now we would like to go into the next one: "Let thy will be done as in heaven so upon the earth."

"Thy will be done." The *will* here is singular in number. We are often concerned with the many wills of God: What is God's will for that? What is God's will for me? What is God's will for you? However, there is the will of God which we sometimes forget, and it is because we do not know the will of God that we get confused as to the many wills of God. So if we could only know the will of God, it would put everything in the right perspective and help us to understand and know God's will concerning this or that.

God's will is something for which we need to pray. We know that His will shall be done sooner or later, no doubt about that, yet we do find that the Lord involves us in this matter of God's will being done. If we pray for His will to be done, it will hasten its fulfillment. If we do not pray for His will to be done, it may be delayed or postponed. Now what is this will of God that He wants us to pray about? What is the will of the Father? I think it is very clear. The will of the Father is actually only one—His only begotten Son. In

Ephesians and Colossians it may be stated differently, but it comes to the same thing.

It is God's will that His Son shall have first place in all things; that He shall have pre-eminence in all things; that one day all things shall be summed up in Christ; that His Son shall be all and in all; that His Son shall be glorified; that His Son shall inherit all things.

Now we know that His will *will* be done, but we also know there is something upon this earth that is opposing this will. There is not only the archenemy of God—Satan and his kingdom of darkness—there is in our flesh that which also is in opposition to His will. Therefore, we find there is a tremendous spiritual battle over this will of God being done on earth as it is in heaven.

Ephesians 6:10-20 speaks of a warrior and, strictly speaking, that warrior is not an individual but the church of God. The church of God is like a warrior fully armed and ready for battle. In Ephesians 6:13 it says,

> For this reason take to you the panoply of God, that ye may be able to withstand in the evil day, and, having accomplished all things, to stand.

So we see that it is not just to withstand the enemy of God but even to accomplish all things. Notice the footnote in the J. N. Darby translation relating to the phrase, "having accomplished all things." It says: "Or having overcome all things. It is to carry through and put in execution all that is purposed and called for in spite of opposition." The enemy is opposing God's will being done on earth as it is in heaven, and the church is standing with God to withstand the enemy and to carry through and put in execution all that is called for in spite of opposition. It is not just a passive resistance to withstand; it is a positive execution. And this is where the spiritual conflict really is. So how are we going to overcome all things?

> We do not war according to flesh. For the arms of our warfare are not fleshly, but powerful according to God to the overthrow of strongholds; overthrowing reasonings and every high thing that lifts itself up against the knowledge of God, and leading captive every thought into the obedience of the Christ (II Corinthians 10:3-5).

As to this matter of God's will, it is not just something for which we fight. It is also that for which we must pray. It is only by praying, "Thy will be done," that we win the battle, carry through, and put in execution that which is purposed and called for. Therefore, it is of tremendous importance that we, as God's people, take up this matter in prayer.

There are times when we feel we do not know what to pray for; but here we are commanded to pray that His will be done on earth as it is in heaven, that His Son shall have the first place in all things, that all things shall be gathered together unto Him, that He shall be all and in all, and that He shall inherit all things. Sometimes, when we talk about God's will, we take a kind of passive resignation, saying, "Well, if it is God's will, may His will be done." This is actually a resigning of ourselves to fate, but this is not what the Scripture says because the Lord says we need to pray for God's will. On our part, it must be active. We really need to pray that God's will *will* be done. It is true we do have to yield ourselves to God's will, whatever it may be, but it is not a passive resignation. We have to actively seek and pray, giving ourselves to God's will that it may be done. It is an active co-operation, and we should pray for it.

Let us recall Jesus and His time in the garden of Gethsemane. That was the most holy hour and so sacred a scene that it is almost beyond words, but what was the prayer of our Lord?

> My Father, if it be possible let this cup pass from me; but not as I will, but as thou wilt (Matthew 26:39b).

The Lord Jesus was actively praying for the Father's will to be done; it was not just a passive resignation. He really prayed earnestly and with such fervency that His sweat came down like drops of blood. In other words, He was seeking desperately for God's will to be done on earth as it is in heaven because there was a tremendous conflict over God's will. The enemy was trying very hard to dissuade, as it were, the Lord. Even the holy human nature of our Lord Jesus shrank back from the very thought that He was going to be made sin— He who knew no sin would be made sin for us. Yet our Lord said, "If it be possible let this cup pass from me, but not as I will, but as thou wilt." He positively prayed for God's will to be done and it was done.

Therefore, I do feel this is something which we need to take up: "Thy will be done on earth as it is in heaven." The Holy Spirit will apply God's will to different matters; He will do the interpretation as we pray for different things. Some people think that if we say, "If it is Your will, may it be done," then that means you do not have faith. If you have faith, you should say, "Lord, do this or do that." Now, what about Jesus praying: "Not My will but Thine be done"? Did He not have faith? He had full confidence in His Father, and He wanted His Father's will to be done.

If we know what God's will is, yes, we may pray with confidence. We can say, "Lord, this is Your will; therefore, we stand with You; we want Your will to be done." But, if we do not know what the will of God is, I do not think it is a lack of faith if we say, "Lord, if it is possible, let this be done, but not my will but Thine be done." This is not a lack of faith; on the contrary, it is faith because we believe that God's will shall be done.

"Let Thy will be done as in heaven so upon the earth." The degree of God's will being done is to be no less than it is done in heaven. We know it is done in heaven one hundred percent fully, and we want God's will to be done one hundred percent fully on earth as well. Sometimes God's will may be done thirty percent or sixty percent, but we need to pray that it should be done one hundred percent on earth as it is in heaven. This is where we really need to stand with God in prayer.

So when God's people come together to pray, it is not just that we are asking God to do something for us according to what we would like Him to do. That is not prayer. When we are praying, actually, we stand with God that His will be done on earth as it is in heaven. No matter what subject we touch upon, this is the basic principle: God's will and not ours. We can express to Him what we would like Him to do according to our understanding, but we do not want just that; rather, we desire it to be according to His understanding.

As we pray in whatever areas or subjects we touch upon, may the Lord help us to stand with Him for *His* will to be done.

35—Daily Bread

Matthew 6:11—Give us today our needed bread.

As we continue to consider this prayer which the Lord taught His church to pray, we see that He wants us to pray that God's needs are met before we pray for our own. This is the order. Often, we forget that God has needs because we are so completely wrapped up with our own. When we come to Him we just begin with our own needs, forgetting His altogether. This is probably one reason our needs are not met. If we could see that we should pray for God's needs first, then when we pray for our own, they would be met.

In Matthew 6:33, our Lord said, "But seek ye first the kingdom of God and His righteousness, and all these things shall be added unto you." The Lord wants us to seek the kingdom of God and His righteousness first, and, of course, this seeking includes prayer; so that is why we feel that the church needs to pray for God's name, for God's kingdom, and for God's will.

I do not feel it is a contradiction that the Lord would teach us to pray "give us today our needed bread." We just read in the word that when we are seeking His kingdom and His righteousness, all these things shall be added unto us. Sometimes, we may wonder if daily bread is included in all these things because immediately before that, the Lord said, "Be not therefore careful, saying, What shall we eat? or What shall we drink? or What shall we put on? for your heavenly Father knows that ye have need of all these things" (Matthew 6:31,32b). Does seeking the kingdom first mean that we do not need to pray for all these things? Well, He did say, "All these things shall be added unto you," but He did not say they will be added unto you without prayer. In other words, sometimes these things will be added to you without your even praying, but at other times, you will need to pray for them. It is just a matter of keeping the right order. We must pray for God's needs first, and then we may pray for ours because the kingdom of God is the basic; daily bread is additional. If we forget the basic and just go right to the additional, it may not be added; but if we go to the basic, then we may pray for that addition, and we will find it shall be added unto us. Therefore, it does not mean we should not pray for our daily bread. As a matter of fact, we should because the Lord teaches the church this prayer. I wonder how much the church really has prayed this prayer, "Give us this day our daily bread." Sometimes we may think, "It seems a lack of faith or trust to pray such a prayer," or we may feel when we get to the physical and material things, they are not too spiritual. Perhaps it is because the church has not been praying this prayer that we find problems in this age. The Lord teaches and instructs us to pray this prayer, and it is for the church to take up. I believe there are several reasons why we should pray this prayer.

First, we are living in a very hostile world, and it is not easy for Christians to live a righteous and godly life. In other words, we are living in enemy territory, and the atmosphere around us is hostile and opposing. If we want to be faithful to the Lord and live a righteous and godly life, how we need to look to our heavenly Father to support us and supply us with all our needs. One day will find that "no one will be able to buy or sell save he that had the mark, the name of the beast, or the number of its name" (Revelation 13:17). Even these physical things will be under such control that for people to live godly and righteously, it will mean starvation and physical death. It will mean lack, and these days are coming. In a sense, we are already in those days, and because of that, the church should pray for daily bread. We must look to our heavenly Father to supply our necessities; otherwise, we will find the enemy trying to take away even those things.

Secondly, praying this kind of prayer creates within us a spirit of dependence, and, as Christians, we need to cultivate this. We may think, "I earn my own bread." It is true we have to work, as the Bible says, "If any man does not like to work, neither let him eat" (II Thessalonians 3:10b). But that does not mean that because we work, we earn our daily bread. If the Father does not give us our daily bread, no matter what we may do, we will not have it. Because we depend on ourselves, we forget this. We feel that since we have a job and work very diligently, we therefore earn our own bread. We feel as if this is the way we have our livelihood or our support. We must be reminded that our heavenly Father gives, and then we are fed. If He does not give, we will not have any regardless of how hard we work. He is the One who gives to us and seeing that creates within us a spirit of dependence and thankfulness. That is why we pray before we eat. It is not because it is a formality that we do it. It is that we acknowledge that our daily bread is given to us by our heavenly Father.

Thirdly, this also helps to cultivate within us a sense of trust. As we go on and the days become more and more evil, this sense of trusting the heavenly Father should increase. We really need to trust for our every need. We may not think prayer is necessary since we have food, but we must remember that there are people in this world, even within the household of God, that have to look to the Father for their daily bread. That is the reason this is the church's prayer. As the church of God, we should not be so self-centered because we do not have this need at the present moment, and, therefore, we do not pray this prayer. We must remember there are brothers and sisters who are literally praying for their daily bread, and we should, as God's church, stand with them.

Fourthly, it builds an attitude of contentment. "Give us today our daily bread." We are not asking for abundance or luxury; we are only asking for daily bread—not for tomorrow, but for today.

But godliness with contentment is great gain (I Timothy 6:6).

The problem with the world today is that people are never content. They always want more and more, and therefore they are tempted and fall into destruction. As God's people, when we pray this prayer, it helps us be truly content with daily needs, and it builds within us this attitude of contentment. I do feel it is the will of God that His church should pray this prayer.

It is true that when our Lord Jesus was on earth, He was always looking after the basic—preaching the word, trying to supply the spiritual need—but He also used five loaves and two fishes to feed the five thousand. He was compassionate and considerate, and thus He took care of the needs of the people. Now certainly, the Lord wants us to be compassionate and considerate. We may only have five loaves and two fishes, but the Lord can multiply and feed five thousand. So I feel that when the Lord teaches us to pray such a prayer, it is not, in any sense, that we are to forget God's needs and fall so low as to only see our physical needs. I believe that the Lord truly cares for us and promises us that if we seek His kingdom and righteousness first, these things shall be added to us.

Sometimes when we read biographies of God's people throughout the centuries, we realize that many of them had to pray for their daily bread. As they did this, the Lord answered, which created within them a deep sense of daily looking to the Lord and dependence upon Him. In one sense, we may think that kind of life is very difficult, but then again, it is really glorious. They came to know the Lord in such a personal, intimate way, seeing that He really took care of every small thing in their lives. It is a real blessing.

Therefore, I do feel that it is not forbidden to pray for our daily bread; on the contrary, we are commanded to do so. Remember, it is the prayer of the church; and even if we do not have this immediate need today, somewhere God's people have such a need. As I have said before, if we pray such a prayer, it will do us good in a spiritual way since it creates within us trust, contentment, and a looking to the Lord. It keeps us from becoming forgetful and self-reliant, thinking that we made it all. This will help us to look to the Father and draw us nearer to Him. May the Lord help us in this matter.

36—Forgive Us Our Debts

Matthew 6:12—And forgive us our debts, as we also forgive our debtors.

We have mentioned that we have three petitions at the beginning of the so-called Lord's prayer which are concerned with God's interests. We must always take God's interest as the first and foremost thing for which to pray. Then there are three more petitions which pertain to our needs or our interest. So after we pray for God's interest, then we are able to pray for that which concerns us. The three petitions for our own needs will cover every need which we have while we are on earth waiting for the return of the Lord.

"Give us today our needed bread" or our physical need. Bread is basically our relationship with our heavenly Father because we look to Him for the supply of our daily needs.

"And forgive us our debts, as we also forgive our debtors." This is our soulical or psychological need. This is primarily our relationship with our fellow man.

"And lead us not into temptation, but save us from evil." This is our spiritual need. It has reference to the evil one—that is, we ask the Lord to deliver us from him.

This prayer—"Forgive us our debts, as we also forgive our debtors"—is the only petition with a condition. This is not a sinner's prayer. If it were, there would be no condition. When we cry out for mercy as a sinner, God hears us and forgives us. It is on the basis of the shed blood of our Lord Jesus and is not conditional upon what we do. Therefore, when we come to God and ask for forgiveness by believing in the Lord

Jesus, our sins are forgiven, our debts are all paid off. God does not lay down any condition for us to fulfill before He will forgive us, and we thank God for that because if He should we would not get forgiveness. It is as the hymn says: "Jesus Paid It All." When we come to God through Jesus Christ, our sins are forgiven unconditionally because Jesus has paid it all. But we see a difference here in this request to be forgiven. Our being forgiven is conditional upon our forgiving others. In other words, if we do not forgive others, God will not forgive us. Therefore, this is not a sinner's prayer; it is the prayer of the church. After we come to the Lord Jesus and receive mercy and forgiveness within the context of the church, God expects us to exhibit the same compassion and mercy which He has shown us. If we do not, then He will not forgive our debts.

Most likely, if we think about it, we dare not pray this prayer. We might recite it, but if we really understood what it means, I wonder if we would pray such a prayer, "Forgive us our debts, as we also forgive our debtors." Once a lady wrote to Campbell Morgan after he talked on the Lord's prayer, saying that she changed the words a little bit in her prayer. This is what she said:

"Forgive us our debts,

and we will forgive our debtors."

In other words, forgive us first, and then we will forgive others. She asked if such change was all right. Of course, he wrote back and said it was not right because the Bible says,

"Forgive us our debts,

as we also forgive our debtors."

An unforgiving spirit is very unhealthy to our soul. God wants us to have a healthy, sound soul. He wants us to really have peace in our hearts and rest in our souls, but if we do not forgive, then our unforgiveness will actually hurt our own souls. It may hurt others, but it may hurt us at the same time. Therefore, God wants us to always have a forgiving spirit. If we forgive others, then He will forgive us.

On the one hand, when we come to our heavenly Father, we come with boldness. We approach the throne of grace boldly because of the blood of the Lamb, the blood of the Lord Jesus who has opened a new and living way for us and who is interceding for us as our High Priest. Therefore, when we think of what the Lord has done for us, we can come to Him boldly and pray, but at the same time, when we think of ourselves, we cannot help but feel that we owe Him so much. No one can come to God and feel he does not owe Him anything; we always owe Him because we come short of His glory. Even the best we have is below His standard. In other words, as we come to Him, we realize how much we owe Him. We owe Him glory, honor, praise, worship, and love. We never come to a place where we can say we owe Him nothing. Since this is true, how much we need to forgive others that we may receive forgiveness for our debts. Otherwise, our prayers will be hindered. It is so vital to the spiritual well-being of our soul, that we, by His grace, learn to forgive others that we may receive forgiveness.

Let us recall the story in Matthew 18:21-35. Peter came to the Lord and said: "My brother sinned against me seven times, and I forgave him. Now, what will You say about that?" The Lord said, "I say not to thee until seven times, but until seventy times seven."

Then the Lord used this parable to illustrate this truth: There was a certain bondslave who owed his master ten thousand talents (over a million dollars). He couldn't pay it back. He said, "Give me more time, and I will pay back," but he could not. The master, out of his compassion, forgave him his debt completely. Then this bondslave went out and met a fellow servant who owed him one hundred denarii (a few dollars). He took hold of him and said, "Pay or else go to jail." His fellow servant pled with him, but he would not listen and put him in jail. This matter was known to the master, who called him back and said: "I forgave you all your debts, and yet you will not forgive." And he was delivered to the tormentors until he paid all that was owed.

In this parable, the Lord is teaching us how we need to forgive others. When we think of how much we owe the Lord, what people owe us is nothing. This is the only condition in the so-called Lord's prayer. Even after the Lord finished teaching this, He further explained and enlarged on this one point. This shows how important it is, and it is a prayer that the church ought to pray. Why? Because today you will find among God's people there is such an unforgiving spirit and bitterness towards one another. God's people are so divided; they fight against each other, devour each other, will not forgive each other; and because of this, the testimony of God suffers tremendously. This unforgiving spirit not only affects others, it affects us. Therefore, it is most important for us today that we should pray this prayer.

How we thank God that we can forgive others! Why is it so? It is because His life and His Spirit is within us. If we do not have His life and His Spirit is not within us, we do not have the strength or the willingness to forgive others. His life is a forgiving life; His Spirit is a Spirit of forgiving, and with His life and Spirit within us, we are able to forgive our debtors. And that is grace. Because we are able to forgive our debtors, we will receive forgiveness from God. God wants His people to not only be a *forgiven* people but also a *forgiving* people. We have been forgiven much, so let us now forgive much. If we do, we will be forgiven much more.

Again, let me emphasize that this is not a sinner's prayer because if we confuse it with that, it would seem as if forgiveness would be based on our forgiving others, and that is not true. It is the church's prayer. After we come to the Lord and have all our debts paid and all the past forgiven, then God expects us to be merciful as He is merciful and forgiving as He is forgiving. So we hope that in our prayer, we will not forget or skip the importance of forgiving others.

37—Lead Us Not Into Temptation

Matthew 6:13—And lead us not into temptation, but save us from evil.

This is the last of the three petitions for ourselves. As we mentioned before, we have physical needs, so we need to pray, "give us today our needed bread" (Matthew 6:11). We have soulical needs, so we need to pray, "forgive us our debts, as we also forgive our debtors" (v. 12). We have spiritual needs, so we must pray, "Lead us not into temptation, but deliver us from evil." We live in a hostile world. We are strangers and sojourners, but one thing that really comforts our heart is that our God is sovereign and He rules and overrules everything. Even though evil is upon this earth, yet we know that without our Father's permission, nothing can fall upon us.

God has not promised us that we will not be tempted. In James 1, we are told that God cannot be tempted by evil things, neither does He tempt anyone. Temptation comes from the enemy. The enemy tries to tempt us to sin and, because there is the lust of the flesh within us, we can be enticed and fall into sin. However, without God's permission, even the tempter cannot tempt us. In other words, God sets a limit. He rules even in this matter of temptation, and that is the reason we can pray, "Lead us not into temptation, but deliver us from the evil one." God cannot be tempted, but we, as human beings, can be tempted. Remember that familiar verse:

No temptation has taken you but such as is according to man's nature (I Cor. 10:13).

In other words, man's nature is a fallen one. In this fallen nature, there is lust; therefore, we can be tempted, and we will be tempted. The wonderful thing is, "And God is faithful, who will not suffer you to be tempted above what ye are able to bear." As far as man's nature is concerned, we are exposed to temptation, and we will be tempted. We give ground to the enemy to tempt and attack us, but God is faithful in that He will not allow us to be tempted above that which we are able to bear. Because He knows how much we are able to bear, it is only within that limit that He will allow us to be tempted. Now that is the faithfulness of God. If God allows us to be tempted without setting any limit, how can we stand? But He has set a limit to the temptation that will come upon us. Even though we have ground within us for the enemy to tempt us nevertheless, God sets a limit through His faithfulness. If He does allow us to be tempted, He will always "with the temptation make the issue also."

Here are these two things: (1) He will not suffer us to be tempted above that which we are able to bear. He knows just how much we can stand. (2) As we are being tempted or we are in the process of temptation, He will always make an exit or escape for us. He will always open a way for us to escape from falling or from evil. God promises this to us. He does not promise us that we will not be tempted. He does not tempt us, but He does not promise us that we will not be tempted. Temptation comes from the enemy and because there is lust within us, yet God is so faithful that He rules and overrules in the whole matter of temptation.

Why does God allow us to be tempted sometimes? In the case of Job, Satan asked permission from God to tempt him, and God gave it because, unknown to Job and yet known to God, there was some ground or some impurity there. Therefore, God gave the permission for Satan to tempt Job, but God set a limit and also made an exit for him. The result was that through the temptation, Job was purified. In a sense, God used Satan to purify Job, and sometimes that is the same reason He allows us to be tempted. Even though the thought of the enemy is evil when he tempts us, yet God's thought about it is good—that out of the temptation, we may become stronger than ever before.

There is no reason that we should fall when we are tempted, but if we do, it simply means that we do not look to God. Enough measure of Christ has been planted in us by God to endure the temptation. God knows about it; He has measured it. So if we fall, it is simply because we do not draw upon that which He has already put in us. There is really no excuse if we fall into temptation because it is within God's control.

When our Lord Jesus was on earth, He was tempted in all things in like manner as we are, except sin. Now we are tempted because we have lust within us, unlike the Lord Jesus, who, although He was tempted in all things, did not have that lust within Him. Why was He tempted? In Hebrews, we are told that He suffered being tempted that He might sympathize with us and be a help to us. In other words, we are tempted because of our lust, but He was tempted because of us—not because of himself. God allowed Him to be tempted, and the Spirit even led Him into the wilderness to be tempted by the devil. It was not because of anything in

Him; it was because He was going to be that High Priest, that help to us. Through these temptations, He did not sin; therefore, He is able to deliver us from evil whenever we are tempted.

The prayer here is: "lead us not into temptation," as if God leads us into temptation. What is really meant by this? If we do not pray this prayer, will we have more temptations than will be necessary? Probably, we will, and that is the reason we need to pray this prayer. Sometimes, we can be so bold, thinking that we are able to stand. We become self-confident, presumptuous. We think we are able to meet any temptation. We become careless, but notice the verse in I Corinthians 10:12: "So that let him that thinks that he stands take heed lest he fall." (Also, note that this verse is just before verse 13, which we have been sharing.) When we pray "lead us not into temptation," there is created within us a spirit of humility. It is a holy caution. We should not be presumptuous. Knowing ourselves and what is within us, knowing our flesh in which there is no good, and knowing our human nature, we need to pray to the Lord that He will not lead us into temptation lest we fail to stand. So this kind of prayer is necessary. It keeps us from being self-confident.

Remember how Peter said: "Lord, if everyone leave You, I never will. I am willing to die with You." Well, Satan asked for him and God gave the permission. Peter was sifted, but thank God, at the same time, the Lord said: "I prayed for you; I have asked for you also. Satan asked to sift you, but I asked that your faith fail not. Even though you fall, yet your faith will not fail. You will be recovered." Sometimes we expose ourselves, as it were, to temptation, but knowing how fragile and weak we are, we need to pray this prayer of protection. If we have a humble spirit before the Lord, I do believe that many temptations will be avoided, but if they are necessary (sometimes God thinks temptations are necessary), God will use that temptation to complete us and then deliver us from evil. Even if we are being tempted, yet we will not commit evil. We will not fall into the trap of the enemy. Save us from evil.

When our Lord Jesus was in the garden of Gethsemane, listen to what He prayed: "Father, if it be possible, let this cup be removed from Me [lead us not into temptation], but if it is Thy will, Thy will be done [deliver us from evil]." I believe that we, as God's people, the church of God, need to pray the same prayer: "Lead us not into temptation, but save us from evil."

Thank God, He is in control; He will hear our prayer, and we will escape many temptations which are not really necessary. In the temptations that are needed, we will find that He will keep us from evil so that we are able to withstand and stand. Also, we will become stronger after we are tempted, just as it was with our Lord Jesus when He came back from the wilderness; He was full of the power of the Holy Spirit. The same thing will be our portion. Very often, because we do not pray this prayer, we are exposed to many unnecessary temptations. Also, we tend to fall into evil, but He is well able to save us from evil. When He allows temptation, He knows He has deposited enough in us to overcome evil.

May the Lord help us.

38—Hallowed Be Thy Name

Matthew 6:9—Thus therefore pray ye: Our Father
who art in the heavens, let thy name be sanctified.
(Hallowed be Thy Name—King James Version)

In this prayer that our Lord teaches His church to pray,
we find there are altogether six petitions. Prayer includes
many aspects, and one of them is petition or asking. The first
petition which our Lord teaches His church to pray is
"Hallowed be Thy name." We know that an unbeliever will
not pray. Believers will pray, but oftentimes, when we pray,
we put ourselves and our needs first. Only a believer who lives
in the spirit of the Sermon on the Mount will make
"Hallowed be Thy name" the first and foremost petition.
When we offer our petition to the Lord, do we make known
our own needs first and maybe later think of His needs? I
think that will really reveal where we are.

A petition is a heart desire. When you try to express your
heart's desire before the heavenly Father, what is the first and
foremost desire of your heart? Is it that the name of our Father
may be sanctified? The word hallowed or sanctified in the
Scripture simply means "to be made whole, to be set apart."
Is this really the first desire of our heart? In a very real sense,
His name is holy no matter what, but whether that name is
sanctified on earth, sanctified among His own people, or
sanctified in the world, is a problem. That is the reason such
a petition needs to be offered to our heavenly Father.

A name represents the very person. The petitions, "Thy
kingdom come, Thy will be done on earth as it is in heaven,"

are important, but His name is more intimate and is the sum total of what He is. It is more than kingdom, more than will. It is himself. Where His name is, there will be His presence because His name represents His Person.

Do we really desire that His Person be sanctified? He is holy; He is uncommon; He is unique; He is alone; none can compare with Him. That is what He is. But the question is: Is this true on earth today? Is it true among His own people, in His church? Is it true in this world that is rightfully His? It is the heart desire of the church on earth that the name of the Father be hallowed. When we are praying that prayer, of course, we expect the answer to be fulfilled first in us because unless His name is hallowed among His own people, how can you expect it to be sanctified in the world that does not know Him? Let us ask ourselves and be honest before the Lord: Do we really want His name to be sanctified in our lives? Is this really the first and foremost desire of our heart? This is what it should be because it is the way the Lord teaches us to pray— not our needs first, but His name sanctified first. So I do believe that when we come together to pray as His people, the first and foremost desire of our heart, as we offer our petition, should always be related to His name or to His Person. We want Him to be honored, to be exalted in whatever things we may pray for, and the reason we offer such a petition first is that this is our heart's desire. Otherwise, it will be hypocritical; it will be false. Therefore, we must see that this is truly our heart's desire above all things. We are not interested, in the first place, in ourselves being spiritual. We are not interested in anything else, even our work. Our first and foremost concern is with His name being honored and sanctified, and for this reason, we offer our petition.

Also, we offer such a petition because we know we have no way to fulfill our heart's desire. We want Him to be sanctified, but we cannot sanctify Him. We will find that we will drag His name down. We do not have the spiritual strength to really hallow His name. On the contrary, we find how His name is being put to shame and reproach because of His people. This happened not only with the children of Israel, but it has happened with His church throughout the centuries. That is why we have to offer this petition because we know, in ourselves, there is no way. We have to ask Him to do it.

We offer this petition because we fully believe that He is able to do it. We also believe that as we pray, He will answer; He will give grace, wisdom, and everything that is needed for the realization of this petition. We know that we are called by His name, and that is a tremendous thing because He has committed His name to us; therefore, we are responsible for the sanctity of that name. In a sense, He does require this from us—that we sanctify His name in our lives, in our work, in our homes, in our relationships, and in every area, both together and individually. I would say this is our first responsibility, and because of this, we have to offer this petition; otherwise, there is no way for us to fulfill it.

In a practical way, what does it mean to "let His name be hallowed"? It means putting Him first and letting Him have the first place in our lives, both individually and together. It means that we hear Him; we hearken to Him; we listen to Him; we wait upon Him; we seek to know His will; we are willing to do His will whatever the cost; we yield ourselves to Him that His name may be glorified.

This is one thing which we can see in the life of our Lord Jesus. It is not petition to Him; it is reality. Throughout His life, the Name of the Father was honored; the Name of the Father was sanctified; the Name of the Father was above all. It governed His whole life, even if it meant death. Today He gives His Name to us and expects us to do likewise. So I do feel that as we come to pray, we come to our Father. We do not come to One who is distant, hard, demanding and unreasonable. We come to "Father," but our Father is in the heavens. He is all-wise, all-mighty, and as we come to Him and pour out our heart's desire, we believe He will answer us.

We really need to pray this first petition—"Hallowed be Thy Name"—which our Lord taught His church to pray.

39—Ask the Father In My Name

John 16:23-24—And in that day ye shall demand
nothing of me: verily, verily, I say to you, Whatsoever
ye shall ask the Father in my name, he will give you.
Hitherto ye have asked nothing in my name: ask, and
ye shall receive, that your joy may be full.

When the Lord was on earth with His disciples, no doubt
they frequently asked of Him whenever they had problems or
needs. Also, being Jews, no doubt they prayed to God as the
Maker, the Creator of man. It was really through the death
and resurrection of our Lord Jesus that these disciples were
being brought into a new relationship with God; although,
before the death and resurrection of Jesus, He taught His
disciples to pray, "Our Father, who art in heaven" (see
Matthew 6:9). This relationship, however, was not really
sealed until His resurrection, after which He gave this first
message to the disciples: "But go to my brethren and say to
them, I ascend to my Father and your Father, and to my God
and your God" (John 20:17). So in a sense, we find that this
relationship of having God as Father really came from the
Lord Jesus and was sealed through His death and
resurrection. This is the meaning of His saying, "in that day."
What is that day? It is the day of His resurrection, and today
we are still in that day. The Lord said, "In that day, a great
change will come into your life, even into your prayer life." In
the past, they may have asked the Lord himself whenever they
were in need, and they prayed to God, but the Lord said, "In

that day whatsoever ye shall ask of my Father in my name, He will give you." This was a great change! They could go to God as Father and ask in the name of the Lord Jesus. That was something they had never done before, and this was made possible through the death and resurrection of our Lord.

"In that day ye shall ask in my name; and I say not to you that I will demand of the Father for you." Now it does not mean that from that day onward, the Lord would not pray for His disciples. Of course, He is our Intercessor, He is our High Priest, and He is praying for us. Nevertheless, now the Lord was giving His own a privilege which they had never enjoyed before. They could go to God and pray to Him, not just as God but as Father. Also, they could ask the Father, not in their own name, but in the name of the Lord Jesus, and if they did, the Father would answer them. Why is this so? It is because a name represents that person. When the Lord was still on earth, they did not need to ask in that name; but since the Lord was leaving them, He left His name with them, and His name is as good as His presence. So when the disciples asked the Father in His name, it simply meant that it was as if the Lord himself was asking the Father. That is really what is meant here. When you ask in His name, it means the same as if He is asking and that is the reason the Lord says, "Ask and ye shall receive" (see Matthew 7:7).

Let us consider the Lord Jesus in the case where He called Lazarus out of death. "And Jesus lifted up his eyes on high and said, Father, I thank thee that thou hast heard me; but I knew that thou always hearest me" (John 11:41b, 42a). The Father always hears the Son; He never refuses Him. That is the privilege, the right of the Son towards the Father. So the Lord said: "I give My name to you and you may go to the

Father and ask in My name, just as if I am asking the Father, and He always hears you. He cannot but hear you." That is the power of that name.

We thank God the Lord has given His name to us, and we can come to the Father and ask in His name, but let us remember that using His name is not just a magic word or formula. Oftentimes, when we pray, we say: "in Your name," or "in the name of the Lord Jesus." It means that we do not come in our own name. We cannot come on our own. We come in the name of the Lord Jesus and present our petitions in His name, and we usually conclude our prayer with "in His name," but it can become a kind of formula. We say it, but how much do we really mean it? It is not a magic word; it is not a formula. It is a reality, and because it is, therefore, when we ask in His name, we need to be sure that we ask as He would have asked. If we ask in a way that He would not, then we are using His name in vain. Thus, when we pray in His name, we need to be very careful that we are praying according to His will and for His glory. We are not just asking for a selfish purpose or according to our own idea, but we pray in humility that our prayer will be according to His will so far as we know. Sometimes, we may pray in a way that may not be His will, but so far as we know, we humbly present our petition to our Father in the name of the Lord Jesus as if the Lord himself is praying to the Father. This is the assurance, the confidence that we have because if we pray in His Name to the Father, we will find that He answers us that our joy may be full. So we do thank the Lord for giving us such a great privilege.

Let us realize what a great responsibility this is. We need to pray as if He is praying, and this can only be done through the indwelling Holy Spirit. How do we know that we are praying as He would have prayed? Thank God the Holy Spirit dwells in us, and He will pray according to His will. So let us just look to the Lord. Whenever we come together to pray, we need to know that we cannot pray. We do not know how to pray or what to pray for. But thank God, the Holy Spirit comes to our aid. As we learn to depend on Him and open ourselves to Him, we believe that the indwelling Holy Spirit will pray according to His will. Then, how pleased the Father will be in answering the prayer of His own people.

This does not mean that Christ will not pray for us. He is still praying for us as our High Priest; probably, He will pray for us even more than ever before. But He has given us such a right and privilege, and we need to exercise it and come and pray.

40—Active Involvement in Prayer

Matthew 14:14-21—And going out he saw a great crowd, and was moved with compassion about them, and healed their infirm. But when even was come, his disciples came to him saying, The place is desert, and much of the day time already gone by; dismiss the crowds, that they may go into the villages and buy food for themselves. But Jesus said to them, They have no need to go: give ye them to eat. But they say to him, We have not here save five loaves and two fishes. And he said, Bring them here to me. And having commanded the crowds to recline upon the grass, having taken the five loaves and the two fishes, he looked up to heaven, and blessed: and having broken the loaves, he gave them to the disciples, and the disciples gave them to the crowds. And all ate and were filled, and they took up what was over and above of fragments twelve handbaskets full.

(This message was given on the occasion of purchasing a larger meeting place. Although it addresses specific issues related to the process of that purchase, it is included here because it contains principles that could be of help to all God's people.)

Now you may wonder why I read this passage, but here is a very important principle in regard to prayer. I know we are all thankful and even joyful for what the Lord did last week in giving us a new place where we can meet. There is no question but that the Lord did it. It was the Lord who inclined the hearts of the bankers; it was the Lord who arranged everything; and it was the Lord who gave that place to us that we may use it for Him.

The matter, of course, is not settled yet. For closing, we need $65,000, and the date has been set for December 31, or it can be earlier. Where should we look for this amount of money? I feel we can do it two ways: We can look at it passively; that is, since the Lord has done so marvelously in giving us that property, we can expect Him to drop the $65,000 from heaven. He can rain the money upon us because that is just the remainder. Or we can fall back on the word of the banker who promised that he would allow us to take a mortgage. Now that is the way to approach this matter passively. I believe, however, there is another way the Lord would have us go, and that is to approach it actively. In the matter of the exchange of the properties, the Lord moved sovereignly. But I feel that in the case of the remainder which needs to be supplied, because we, His people, are involved, He will not move independently—that is to say, He will not rain upon us $65,000 because there is a principle involved. (And it is still the Lord who wants to do a miracle.) The principle is He wants us to be actively involved, and that is the reason I read this passage.

There was a great multitude there, and towards evening the disciples came to the Lord and said, "Dismiss the crowds, that they may go into the villages and buy food for themselves." The Lord replied, "They have no need to go: give ye them to eat." He did not say, "I will give them to eat." He said, "You give them to eat." The disciples were thinking of taking the easy way and let them go to the villages; let them look somewhere else. They did not want to be involved; it was too much for them; however, the Lord would not allow it. He wanted them to be involved in something impossible. The disciples said: "We have only five loaves and two fishes. It is just enough for a lunch." How could that possibly feed 5000 men—women and children not counted?

Of course, the Lord knew what He was going to do. He could rain manna from heaven, as He did with the children of Israel in the wilderness (and He did that for forty years). It was a large supply! He could easily have fed five thousand people one supper, but He did not do it. He said, "Give ye them to eat." But the disciples could only find five small loaves and two small fishes. The Lord said, "Bring them here to Me." And when they were in His hands, He took them, blessed them, broke them, and gave to the disciples. The disciples gave to the people, and five thousand men ate and were filled, and afterward, twelve baskets full were left over.

Now that was a miracle, and it was done by the Lord with His own people. I do believe that as we are looking forward to possessing that place, the Lord does not want us to take possession of it in a passive way, expecting the Lord to do everything without us being involved. I feel the Lord intentionally left a remainder to get us involved. He can give us the house. It is possible. Why not? He has already done the greater part; He can easily do the lesser. However, I feel there is something which God wants us to be involved with—the impossible.

Now, what do we have? We know that it is very easy to look at people, but I do not believe that is the attitude we should take. I think the Lord is expecting every one of us to come to Him and inquire as to what He wants us to do. We have five loaves and two fishes, but what will that be with five thousand people? It is nothing, so why not just eat them ourselves? But the Lord can use them. Do not despise the five loaves and two fishes. I think it is a blessing when every one of us can go to the Lord and inquire of Him, asking what He wants each of us to do. The five loaves and two fishes do not seem to be much, but the Lord is not merely looking for "much" because if we have "much," then there is not any need to multiply. The Lord would not be involved. He wants to be involved with us, so what is needed at this moment is for each of us to inquire of Him. Do not look at your brothers and sisters and try to figure things out. Be before the Lord, and when we are willing to give our five loaves and two fishes to Him, He will multiply it.

Oftentimes, when we are faced with such a problem, we throw our hands up, saying we do not have the means to meet the need. Therefore, we either expect the Lord to do it all, or we look around for help—go to the villagers. But that is not the Lord's way. His way is for everyone to be before Him, and when we are faithful to the Lord, we will see His miracle. The reason He wants us to be involved is that He really honors us. He does not want us to be spectators; He wants us to be a part of His own doing. It is a great honor that He should give us such an opportunity to be involved with Him to see what He can do.

I believe it has to do with our prayer. What is the use of continuing to pray, asking the Lord to give us the remaining funds in order that we may close the settlement, while we just look to Him, look to other people and not get ourselves committed? I honestly do not believe the Lord will do anything if we are not committed and do not give, but if we do this, we will see a miracle. We will see how the Lord multiplies and also how much will be leftover.

I feel I must share this with you because it is urgent. The time is very short. If we do not go to the Lord and really stand in the right position before Him, I am afraid when the time comes, we will have to enter into it in a passive way, and that is not honoring the Lord. Therefore, since we are praying for this matter, I think the Lord really expects us to have the right attitude, and if this is so, our prayers will be answered. That is why I have said it has something to do with prayer.

Do not feel that it is a burden or weight. It is not. I feel that it is a privilege. It is an honor that the Lord would call us to work with Him. After everything is done, we will have to say, "It is the Lord," but He wants us to be involved in it.

May the Lord help us as we begin to pray for this matter.

41—Praying for the World Situation

Daniel 4:7—This sentence is by the decree of the watchers, and the decision by the word of the holy ones: that the living may know that the Most High ruleth over the kingdom of men, and giveth it to whomsoever he will, and setteth up over it the basest of men.

When we are praying for the world situation, we know, of course, that what we see is just a front because, behind that which is seen, there is a power in the invisible realm—a power of darkness that actually controls the kingdom of men. For this reason, when we pray for the world situation, we have to go behind the scene and touch the power of darkness that controls man. But I think there is something which we probably neglect when we pray for world situations. We are somehow more occupied with the negative side—the power of darkness working behind the kingdom of men and that this rebellious spirit has to be controlled, restrained, or destroyed. We tend to forget that there is a positive aspect for which we can really stand. In other words, when we are praying for the kingdom of men, that is, the world situation, it is easy for us to approach it from the negative side, praying against the power of darkness that controls the world. But we need to remember that in the word of God, there is a positive side, which is heaven's will.

In this passage in Daniel, it says, "The decree of the watchers and the decision of the word of the holy ones" (see

4:17). Oftentimes, when we touch upon the world situation in our prayer, we neglect this positive side—that is to say, when we are praying, it is more for us to stand for heaven's will than against the enemy's device. Of course, we have to pray against the enemy's device, but I think our approach should be more positive, that is, standing with God for heaven's decree. I think this is something which we should learn and remember.

In this case with Nebuchadnezzar, there was a sentence upon him: "The decree of the watchers and the decision of the word of the holy ones." Who are these watchers? Who are these holy ones? When we think of angelic beings, oftentimes, we think of the fallen angels, and we tend to forget that God has angels who serve Him and His purpose faithfully. So among God's angels, there are those who are called watchers. They watch for God; they watch the kingdom of men; they watch the world situation; they watch individuals; they watch everything that is going on upon this earth. They are watching for God to find out whether things have gone too far, whether things have gone against the will of God, whether things seem to be trying to precipitate before God's time, whether the iniquities are full and God's judgment has to come, or whether there should be a change upon this earth—even the setting up of kings or the overthrowing of authorities.

God has His watchers upon this earth. We do not see them; they are angels, but they are on earth watching what is going on. I believe one very clear instance that we can find is in Genesis 18. Before God destroyed Sodom and Gomorrah, three men came to this earth. One was God himself, and the others were two angelic beings. They came down to find out whether the iniquity was (and it was) very grievous and very bad and whether it was time for God to judge. They came with God to investigate and to find out. These angelic beings are watching, and they will report, as it were, to God for God to act; and the decree of the watchers is actually the decree of God. They represent God in looking over the things upon this earth and then decide for God—or God deciding through them—what He is going to do.

Then there are the holy ones. They are also angelic beings, like the seraphim. You remember in Isaiah 6 the seraphim crying, "Holy, Holy, Holy." They stand for the holiness of God. They are measuring everything and judging everything according to the holiness of God, and when they notice something that is against God's holiness, then they give their word. The word decision, in other versions, can be called "demand." They demand that God's holiness be vindicated. So in the case of Nebuchadnezzar, the watchers were watching him, and the holy ones noticed that the holiness of God was being compromised and needed to be vindicated; therefore, they gave the sentence for Nebuchadnezzar to be driven out for seven years to eat grass as an animal until he humbled himself and realized that the Most High does rule over the kingdom of men (see Daniel 4:23-25).

This is a very important aspect which we need to remember. God has His watchers and holy ones, celestial beings in heaven who are in agreement with Him and who are so one with God that their decree or their decision represents God's decree and God's decision—and that governs what happens upon this earth. In other words, it is not the enemy's device that governs the kingdom of men. It is heaven's decree that governs the kingdom of men.

Where do we come in, and how is it related to prayer? God also has His terrestrial watchers and holy ones. The angels are the celestial watchers and holy ones, but on earth, God has His terrestrial watchers, which is His church. God has set us, His people, as watchers upon this earth, and that is why you will find the Bible says, "Watch and pray." We are to watch what is going on. We are to be alert, and as we are watching, we begin to discern the times. We begin to discern the will of God. We begin to see whether it has gone too far or whether it has gone too fast or whether it is delayed. So as we watch in the Spirit, we really begin to see what is going on.

Also, we are God's holy ones because the word saint means "holy one." We are God's saints; we are holy ones. We are here to stand for the holiness of God. On the one hand, we watch what is going on to see if it is of the will of God. On the other hand, we are here standing for God's holiness; and as we are watching and measuring the things that are going on upon this earth with the holiness of God, I believe we will come to a kind of spiritual knowledge and understanding. Based on that kind of spiritual knowledge and understanding, we pray.

In Matthew 18:18, the Lord said, "Verily I say to you, Whatsoever ye shall bind on the earth shall be bound in heaven, and whatsoever ye shall loose on the earth shall be loosed in heaven." We may think it is the earth that initiates the binding and the loosing, but that is not true because, in the original Greek, it says, "Whatsoever ye shall bind upon this earth shall be having been bound in heaven." Now it is a very strange way of putting it. On the one hand, it is "shall be," but also, "having been." "Shall be having been bound in heaven." So "having been bound or having been loosed in heaven," something has already begun in heaven. In other words, it is God's will; and then people on earth come to know and enter into His will, and when that happens, we will pray accordingly. We bind as it has been bound in heaven, and when we pray and bind, then it shall be bound on earth, and the will of God will be executed upon this earth. The same thing is true with the principle of loosing—having been loosed in heaven.

When we are praying, what we need first of all is to watch. If we are not watching, how can we pray for world situations? We need to watch, but of course, when we watch, we are not just watching the scene. We are watching it with God's interest in our hearts, and we are standing for the holiness of God. It is only when we are watching with such a spirit that we will be able to enter into the mind and heart of God. Then we will begin to know whether it shall be loosed or it shall be bound. This is how we pray for the world situation.

Another thing we can mention is in Ephesians 6. We are involved in a spiritual warfare—we are not fighting against flesh and blood—and that means it is not the scene which we see, but we are battling against the principalities, authorities, the spiritual powers of darkness, and of deception. Yet the Bible says "to withstand" and "to stand." In verse 13, we read, "For this reason take to you the panoply of God that ye may be able to withstand in the evil day." "To withstand" is against the enemy. Concerning the phrase "having accomplished all things," in Darby's footnote, it says, "Or having overcome all things. It is to carry through and put in execution all that is purposed and called for in spite of opposition." In other words, it is not just withstanding evil. In withstanding the evil, you are actually carrying through and executing the purpose of God against all opposition. There is a positive thing going on. It is heaven's decree that is pronounced, heaven's decree that is maintained, and that means to stand and to withstand.

Therefore, if we are praying for the world situation, it is more than just a matter of withstanding; it is a matter of standing. In other words, we are standing together with God for heaven's decree. Even though we are withstanding all the devices of the enemy, there is something very positive in it.

Now, if we know the mind of God, then we can pray more specifically—that is, if we know the mind of God in what heaven has bound, then we can pray for its binding. If we know that the heavens have already loosed it, then we can pray for loosing. But if we do not know, if we have not come to that point yet, then what we can still do is stand for God's will. We can stand for heaven's decree, that it shall be executed upon this or that situation. So I think when we are learning to pray for world situations, which is the kingdom of men, this is a principle which we may go by. It is not a light thing. It is a heavy responsibility, and God expects His people, as watchers and holy ones standing for His holiness and His will, to execute His decree upon this earth.

Here we see the celestial and terrestrial beings working together for God's purpose to be fulfilled upon this earth. It is a very serious thing, and I do believe that if the church, by the power of the Holy Spirit, can really enter into it in the right spirit, then we will find that heaven will have its way upon this earth and the enemy will be overcome.

TITLES AVAILABLE
from Christian Fellowship Publishers
By Watchman Nee

Aids to "Revelation"	Let Us Pray
Amazing Grace	The Life That Wins
Back to the Cross	The Lord My Portion
A Balanced Christian Life	The Messenger of the Cross
The Better Covenant	The Ministry of God's Word
The Body of Christ: A Reality	My Spiritual Journey
The Character of God's Workman	The Mystery of Creation
Christ the Sum of All Spiritual Things	Powerful According to God
The Church and the Work – 3 Vols	Practical Issues of This Life
The Church in the Eternal Purpose of	The Prayer Ministry of the Church
God	The Release of the Spirit
"Come, Lord Jesus"	Revive Thy Work
The Communion of the Holy Spirit	The Salvation of the Soul
The Finest of the Wheat – Vol. 1	The Secret of Christian Living
The Finest of the Wheat – Vol. 2	Serve in Spirit
From Faith to Faith	The Spirit of Judgment
From Glory to Glory	The Spirit of the Gospel
Full of Grace and Truth – Vol. 1	The Spirit of Wisdom and Revelation
Full of Grace and Truth – Vol. 2	Spiritual Authority
Gleanings in the Fields of Boaz	Spiritual Discernment
The Glory of His Life	Spiritual Exercise
God's Plan and the Overcomers	Spiritual Knowledge
God's Work	The Spiritual Man
Gospel Dialogue	Spiritual Reality or Obsession
Grace Abounding	Take Heed
Grace for Grace	The Testimony of God
Heart to Heart Talks	The Universal Priesthood of Believers
Interpreting Matthew	Whom Shall I Send?
Journeying towards the Spiritual	The Word of the Cross
The King and the Kingdom of Heaven	Worship God
The Latent Power of the Soul	Ye Search the Scriptures

The Basic Lesson Series
Vol. 1 - A Living Sacrifice
Vol. 2 - The Good Confession
Vol. 3 - Assembling Together
Vol. 4 - Not I, But Christ
Vol. 5 - Do All to the Glory of God
Vol. 6 - Love One Another

ORDER FROM: 11515 Allecingie Parkway Richmond, VA 23235
www.c-f-p.com